GW00567447

THE MAYA

HISTORY AND TREASURES OF AN ANCIENT CIVILIZATION

WHITE STAR PUBLISHERS

TEXT
DAVIDE DOMENICI

EDITORIAL DIRECTION
VALERIA MANFERTO DE FABIANIS

COLLABORATING EDITOR
LAURA ACCOMAZZO

GRAPHIC DESIGN
PAOLA PIACCO

© 2006 White Star S.p.A.
Via Candido Sassone, 22/24
13100 Vercelli, Italy
www.whitestar.it

TRANSLATION: CATHERINE BOLTON

ISBN-10: 88-544-0148-X
ISBN-13: 978-88-544-0148-8

REPRINTS:
1 2 3 4 5 6   10 09 08 07 06

Printed in Singapore
Color separation: Fotomec, Turin

1 - THIS CHACMOOL STANDS AT THE
ENTRANCE TO THE TEMPLE OF THE
WARRIORS AT CHICHÉN ITZÁ.

2-3 - CLOSE-UP OF AN OLMEC COLOSSAL
HEAD.

4-5 - MURALS AT BONAMPAK.

6-7 - AERIAL VIEW OF THE CASTILLO AT
CHICHÉN ITZÁ.

8 - MASKS OF DEITIES IN THE PUUC MAYA
AREA IN NORTHERN YUCATÁN.

Ever since the mid-1800s, when explorers like John Lloyd Stephens and Frederick Catherwood revealed the existence of splendid ruins buried in the heart of the tropical forests of southern Mexico and Guatemala, the ancient Maya civilization has continued to fascinate scholars and enthusiasts alike. Pyramids and palaces, ornately decorated with sculptures and bas-reliefs, have painted the picture of a rich, sumptuous society ruled by an ambitious and sophisticated elite class, capable of complex mathematical and calendrical notation, but also of war, conspiracy and human sacrifice. Archaeological research has discovered rich tombs, colorful murals and the modest dwellings of peasant families. Likewise, as Maya writing is gradually being deciphered, it continues to reveal new and often surprising aspects of this ancient civilization. Everything about the Maya seems to be marked by a sense of doom and the impending specter of the much-debated but baffling "collapse" that seems to have wiped out these ancient lords of the forest.

All too often, however, the fame of the Maya culture, whose extraordinary artistic output has justly made it one of the ancient world's most renowned civilizations, has overshadowed the achievements of other peoples. Indeed, alongside the Maya these groups played a leading role for several millennia in the history of Mesoamerica, the cultural area that extended from the modern-day territories of central and northern Mexico to Guatemala, Belize, Honduras, El Salvador, and parts of Nicaragua and Costa Rica. First of all, in order to grasp the historical and cultural trajectory of the Maya civilization – particularly its origin and "collapse" – we must examine neighboring populations, above all the ones that were part of the Olmec tradition of the isthmian region. Indeed, the origins of the Olmec culture greatly predate the birth of the Maya civilization. Moreover, we must consider other populations that, though farther away, were no less important, such as the Zapotec, the Teotihuacán and the Aztec, who prospered in the lands northwest of the Maya and Olmec areas. The history of Mesoamerica was the history of all these peoples and of their relationships. It was marked by a continuous dialectical movement between cultural unity and region-

10-11 - VIEW OF PALENQUE BY FREDERICK CATHERWOOD. IN THE MID-19TH CENTURY, CATHERWOOD'S DRAWINGS AND JOHN LLOYD STEPHENS' DESCRIPTIONS CONTRIBUTED TO THE INTEREST THAT THE REDISCOVERY OF THE MAYA CIVILIZATION AROUSED IN EUROPE AND THE UNITED STATES.

al diversity, generating a process that often took on the form of cultural polarity, in which the populations of the tropical lowlands of the Southeast encountered and clashed with those of the Mexican highlands.

This book is about one of these two cultural hubs of Mesoamerica: the large tropical area of the Southeast, where the Olmec and the Maya produced two great cultural traditions engaged in constant dialogue. But who were the Olmec and the Maya? Although the name "Olmec" is used to refer to a specific archaeological culture that developed between 1200 and 400 BC, its descendants, who spoke languages from the Mixe-Zoquean family, occupied the regions of the isthmian region for millennia – and still live there today. This does not mean that over the centuries these isthmian groups felt that they were "Olmec" (in fact, this name is used purely as a convention), but that the isthmian cultural manifestations were part of what, in many ways, can be considered an uninterrupted tradition, albeit one that was characterized by "collapses," revivals and external cultural contributions. The linguistic factor seems to have been decisive in this continuity, given the fact that the speakers of languages related to the tongue spoken by the Olmec still live in Mexico's isthmian regions today. This means that for over 3000 years groups that speak Mixe-Zoquean languages have occupied the coastal wetlands of the Gulf of Mexico (the modern states of Veracruz and Tabasco), western Chiapas, the enormous Grijalva River Valley or Central Depression, and the fertile coastal region of Chiapas and Guatemala, also known as Soconusco. The Maya – meaning the speakers of languages belonging to the Mayance family – still occupy the lowlands of the Yucatán Peninsula, the rainforests of Petén, which are crossed by rivers such as the Usumacinta and Río de la Pasión, and the highlands of Chiapas and Guatemala. Also with reference to the Maya, we cannot refer to a single culture that was the same or united for thousands of years, but to a great cultural tradition with many regional and chronological manifestations.

Thus, we are talking about two great linguistic and cultural traditions that developed for thousands of years in neighboring regions. For centuries these border areas, such as the eastern edge of the Gulf of Mexico, the western portion of the Central Depression, and the transitional areas between the Pacific Coast and the highlands of Chiapas and Guatemala, were areas of cultural interaction, exchange and conflict between the two traditions, and this fact contributed significantly to the region's development as a whole.

Because of this constant interaction and the common environmental characteristics of these areas, the Olmec, Maya and other Mesoamerican populations shared forms of subsistence – based essentially on the cultivation of maize, squash, beans and peppers – and cultural notions concerning cosmology, deities and the perception of time. This "core" of the Mesoamerican cultural tradition developed over thousands of years, starting in about 2500 BC, during which Mesoamerica was dotted with small farming communities. This tradition was then "interpreted" in various ways in the different Mesoamerican regions, populated by groups that were highly diversified both culturally and linguistically. The events of the Olmec and Maya world show that some of the ancient farming villages developed into centers of power, where the rulers of increasingly stratified and complex societies lived. In turn, these societies founded the splendid capitals of chiefdoms and kingdoms that, starting in 1200 BC, dominated the Mesoamerican scenario, producing a millenary history of rises and falls, and of magnificent cultural and artistic developments.

Some of these kingdoms were destined to meet other men from a faraway world: men who rode horses, used firearms and worshipped other deities, and who ultimately vanquished the Indian populations, starting a long period of colonial exploitation. These were centuries of forced labor, cultural and religious oppression, and demographic catastrophes that, even after the Spanish colonies gained their independence, threatened the Indians' very existence. And yet these populations were able to preserve and recreate their own identity in the underground forms of ethnic resistance. In spite of all this, the descendants of the ancient Olmec and Maya still populate the lands of Mesoamerica today, proudly claiming their cultural identity and millenary history: their story is waiting to be told.

13 - This masterpiece of Classic Maya sculpture is part
of the back of one of the carved thrones from the city
of Piedras Negras (Guatemala). Each Maya city had its
own school, generating a stylistic variety that is one of
the most surprising aspects of Maya art
(Amparo Museum, Puebla).

CHRONOLOGY

EARLY PRECLASSIC PERIOD
(2500–900 BC)

The Early Preclassic Period saw the gradual development of agriculture and sedentariness in Mesoamerica, accompanied by slow population growth. Groups living in farm villages mainly established egalitarian societies, but the first forms of social hierarchy arose in the Chiapas area, on the Pacific Coast, in about 1400 BC. The monumental city of San Lorenzo developed on the Gulf Coast in about 1150 BC. The first capital of the Olmec civilization, it was the leading force in the Olmec expansion to the isthmian area.

MIDDLE PRECLASSIC PERIOD
(900–300 BC)

The Middle Preclassic marked the heyday of the Olmec civilization, with the development of the monumental centers of La Venta and Tres Zapotes. The earliest forms of glyphic writing developed in this area. During this period, the Olmec artistic style spread to most of Mesoamerica. At the same time, the first monumental centers were established in various regions of the Maya area, particularly around Belize and in the central lowlands. The most notable include Nakbé and El Mirador, the capitals of the first great centralized states of the Maya world.

LATE PRECLASSIC PERIOD
(300 BC–AD 250)

In the area around the Gulf of Mexico, the Late Preclassic was marked by the breakdown of Olmec domination and the rise of new Mixe-Zoque chiefdoms such as Cerro de Las Mesas and Izapa. Glyphic writing and the calendar system known as the Long Count be-

came widespread here. In the Maya area, the Late Preclassic was a period of extraordinary urban development, in which some of the most important Maya cities flourished, such as Tikal in the central lowlands and Kaminaljuyú in the Guatemalan highlands.

EARLY CLASSIC PERIOD
(AD 250–600)

During the Early Classic, the political entities that arose during the previous period enjoyed an era of great prosperity, not only along the Gulf of Mexico (Cerro de Las Mesas) but also in the Maya area, where Tikal came to dominate most of the central lowlands. The city clashed with the nearby state of Kaan, and countless new royal dynasties were founded throughout the Maya area. The stele/altar complex became the main monumental form in the Maya world, and was associated with the rapid spread of glyphic inscriptions for the purpose of historical records and propaganda. In Central Mexico, Teotihuacán became the largest city of Mesoamerica and the capital of a powerful centralized state.

LATE CLASSIC PERIOD
(AD 600–900)

After the fall of Teotihuacán and the temporary decline of Tikal, the Late Classic was distinguished by the cultural and artistic efflorescence of the Classic societies. Different regional cultures developed around the Gulf of Mexico and along the Pacific coast (central Veracruz, El Tajín). The Maya lowlands became the stage of enormous competition among important cities such as Tikal, Calakmul, Palenque, Yaxchilán and Copán. The end of this period was marked by what has come to be referred to as the "collapse" of the Maya civilization, a sweeping political crisis that led to abandonment of the main cities of the southern lowlands. However, this crisis did not affect the northern Maya areas as profoundly.

EARLY POSTCLASSIC PERIOD
(AD 900 – 1250)

The Early Postclassic was a period distinguished by renewed political balance following the collapse of the Classic Period, and it also marked the beginning of migrations of northern populations that entered Mesoamerica. The first great multiethnic political entities, such as the Toltec capital of Tula, were established during this period, in which there was a sharp decline in the use of writing. The cult of the Feathered Serpent and the legendary city of Tollan spread throughout Mesoamerica, ushering in an era of vast cultural standardization, which is evident with the rise of the state of Chichén Itzá in Yucatán.

LATE POSTCLASSIC PERIOD
(AD 1250–1519)

The dissolution of the vast centralized states of the previous period led to political fragmentation in many Mesoamerican regions. In the Maya area, the state capital of Mayapán rose to rule for about two centuries, followed by a period in which small independent kingdoms developed. On the Gulf Coast, Totonac cities such as Cempoala flourished. In central Mexico, the Mexica founded the city of Tenochtitlan, which gradually came to dominate the local mosaic composed of numerous independent cities, ultimately becoming the capital of the greatest and most powerful empire in the history of Mesoamerica.

BELIZE
HONDURAS
NICARAGUA

MEXICO

SAN SALVADOR

GUATEMALA

✷ DZIBICHALTÚN   ✷ EK BALAM

✷ CHICHÉN ITZÁ

✷ UXMAL

KABAH ✷   COBÁ ✷

✷ LABNÁ   TULUM ✷

SAYIL ✷

✷ EDZNÁ

✷ EL TAJÍN

✷ TEOTIHUACÁN

✷ MEXICO CITY   ✷ CERRO DE LAS MESAS

✷ LAGUNA DE LOS CERROS   CALAKMUL ✷

✷ LA VENTA

SAN LORENZO ✷   ✷ SAN BARTOLO

✷ EL MIRADOR

PALENQUE ✷   ✷ PIEDRAS NEGRAS

TONINÁ ✷   ✷ TIKAL

✷ YAXCHILÁN   ✷ TOPOXTE

TAYASAL ✷

✷ SEIBAL

✷ QUIRIGUÁ

✷ PASO DE LA AMADA

✷ KAMINALJUYÚ   ✷ COPÁN

16-17 - CLOSE-UP OF STELE H FROM
COPÁN, PORTRAYING THE RULER
WAXAKLAJUUN UB'AAH K'AWIIL. MOST
MAYA ART WAS PRODUCED AS
PROPAGANDA, AS IT WAS INTENDED TO
GLORIFY THE RULERS AND THEIR FEATS.

18-19 - THE CITY OF UXMAL, WHICH WAS
ONE OF THE MOST IMPORTANT PUUC
MAYA CITIES ON THE YUCATÁN

PENINSULA, IS DOMINATED BY THE
SHEER SIZE OF THE PYRAMID OF THE
MAGICIAN.

20-21 - THE MAYA WERE THE ONLY
AMERICAN POPULATION TO DEVELOP A
COMPLEX SYSTEM OF GLYPHIC WRITING,
WHICH WAS USED MAINLY TO RECORD
HISTORICAL AND RELIGIOUS
INFORMATION.

1

THE OLMEC AND THE BIRTH
OF THE MAYA CIVILIZATION
(1600–300 BC)

FROM EARLY FARMING COMMUNITIES TO THE FIRST HIERARCHICAL SOCIETIES

The oldest traces of sedentary agricultural populations in southeastern Mesoamerica date back to the Early Pre-classic Period (2500–900 BC). In about 1600 BC groups that spoke Mixe-Zoquean languages established the first villages in Soconusco, the fertile coastal region of Chiapas and Guatemala. The earliest remains of small farm villages, located in the coastal regions of the Gulf of Mexico and along the banks of the Grijalva River that were also settled by Mixe-Zoque groups, date back to about 1400 BC. The location of these ancient farming villages is not surprising: the Pacific Coast, the Grijalva Valley and the Gulf Coast are among the richest regions in Mesoamerica, with fertile soil and plenty of water. The first farming villages of the Maya area were established a few centuries later. They were concentrated mainly in what is now Belize, and along the Motagua Valley in the region of modern-day Guatemala and Honduras.

Clearly, all these farming villages established toward the middle of the 2nd millennium BC did not arise from nothing but developed from earlier groups of hunter-gatherers who learned how to exploit important natural resources, such as shrimp and shellfish from the coastal lagoons. There is no direct evidence of linguistic continuity between the last of the Archaic hunter-gatherers and the first farmers.

Nevertheless, studies in historical linguistics strongly suggest that there was indeed continuity, indicating that proto-Mayan and proto-Mixe-Zoquean languages must have been spoken in southeastern Mesoamerica since at least 2000 BC.

The most important developmental sequence of the early agricultural societies of the Southeast has been discovered in the Soconusco area, along the Pacific coast of Chiapas. Starting in 1600 BC, Mixe-Zoque farming communities flourished here. These farmers supplemented their diet of crops with rich marine resources. They used sophisticated pottery (known as Barra pottery), imported prized goods such as jadeite and obsidian from faraway areas, and even played ball, as demonstrated by the ancient ball court at the site of Paso de la Amada (Chiapas).

It seems that by 1400 BC this combination between control over importation, and political and ritual activities like ball-playing led to the rise of ruling groups whose power had gained hereditary status. Excavations at Paso de la Amada uncovered what seems to have been the residence – reconstructed several times – of one of these lords. These noblemen, who supposedly descended from the gods, dominated the local political scene through networks of alliances and patrons.

These networks were maintained and reinforced by ceremonies for the redistribution of goods such as jadeite, obsidian and *pinole*, a beverage that was made by blending cocoa (Soconusco has always been a leading production area) and maize (imported as an exotic product from the Guatemalan highlands), and served in exquisite Barra pots. A model of stratified society was being formed, and it soon became common in many Mesoamerican regions, particularly the coast of the Gulf of Mexico. This region was occupied by Mixe-Zoquean speakers who apparently had close contact with the linguistically similar region of Soconusco that, at the time, was the most dynamic and innovative in southeastern Mesoamerica. It is clear that, even in this early phase, the isthmus was a linguistically uniform region in which the Soconusco groups, known as the Mokaya, played a key role.

However, the balance of the various regions soon changed. In about 1150 BC, the region around the Gulf of Mexico took on a leading role and directly controlled the Soconusco area, probably through shrewd diplomatic policies and marital alliances. The powerhouse of this new political structure in the southeast was San Lorenzo (Veracruz), the capital of the oldest and most important Olmec chiefdom.

23 - The picture shows Colossal Head No. 6 from San Lorenzo (Veracruz) (National Museum of Anthropology, Mexico City).

24 - Structure 4 at Paso de la Amada, in Chiapas, is the oldest example of a Mesoamerican chieftain's dwelling, and provides evidence of the process of social stratification that began to develop in about 1400 BC among the Mokaya along the Pacific coast.

25 - The Lord of Las Limas (Veracruz), made of jadeite, portrays a ruler holding the image of a were-jaguar, which probably represented the young Maize God (Xalapa Anthropology Museum, Veracruz).

SOCIETY, ECONOMY AND DIET IN ANCIENT MESOAMERICA

Starting in the Preclassic Period, Mesoamerican societies acquired a distinctive hierarchical and stratified organization that varied in complexity but essentially remained the same over the millennia that followed. This organization was reflected in different individual occupations.

In these societies, most of the population worked as farmers, mainly cultivating maize, beans, squash and peppers. These staples were supplemented by meat from domesticated animals such as turkeys, or wild ones like deer, armadillos and a type of small boar known as *jabalí*.

Maize was boiled in limewater to soften the cuticle, and was then ground to make *masa*, a mixture used for various preparations. The most important included different types of water-maize beverages (*atole*, *pozol*, *pinole*) and *tamales*, "loaves" of *masa* that were wrapped in maize husks and steamed in neckless *ollas* known as *tecomates*. Small cakes of ground maize, cooked on a terracotta griddle called a *comal*, became popular in central Mexico toward the end of the 1st millennium AD: the Spaniards later named these cakes tortillas. Various types of vegetable soups were probably an important part of the diet and, like the other foods discussed here, they are still very common in the Mexican diet today.

Subsistence farming was the principal form of agriculture. Each family group was independent from an economic standpoint and food was not traded extensively, with the exception of highly prized items like cocoa beans, which were available exclusively to the noble classes. They were used to prepare a beverage that was poured from one vessel to another from a considerable height, forming a thick froth that was considered the most delectable part.

In these hierarchical societies, farmers – who also worked as artisans – were required to pay the noble classes a tribute in the form of goods and labor. The nobles, who often claimed they were descended from the gods and were exempted from farm work, devoted their time to an array of activities like political and religious administration, artwork, war and the trade of luxury goods, conducted in the form of exchange and without using coinage.

The rigid class differences were reflected in clothing and ornaments, whose use was strictly regulated. For example, only nobility could wear sandals, decorated capes, rich headdresses, and jade and turquoise jewelry. It was very difficult to cross class boundaries. For example, we know that during the Aztec era the only way a commoner could become a nobleman was by going to war, which was considered an extremely important activity. Slavery was rare and economically insignificant. It was limited to prisoners of war and debtors, but in many cases they could regain their freedom.

26 - MAIZE HAS ALWAYS BEEN CONSIDERED THE QUINTESSENTIAL PLANT OF THE MESOAMERICAN CIVILIZATION. THIS MAYA VASE PORTRAYS A WOMAN GRINDING MAIZE, USING THE TYPICAL BASALT GRINDING STONE KNOWN AS A METATE (ISRAEL MUSEUM, JERUSALEM).

27 - THE BODY OF THE CACAO GOD IS COMPOSED OF A HEAP OF SEEDS FROM THIS PLANT. COCOA BEANS, USED TO PREPARE VARIOUS BEVERAGES, WERE RESERVED FOR THE NOBLE CLASSES AMONG THE MAYA (NATIONAL MUSEUM OF ARCHAEOLOGY, GUATEMALA CITY).

28 - The Olmec colossal heads — the one shown here is No. 8 from San Lorenzo (Veracruz) — are probably monumental portraits of the rulers crafted upon their death. The realism of their facial features confirms the fact that they were full-fledged portraits and not idealized images (Xalapa Anthropology Museum, Veracruz).

29 - The Olmec masks, made of semiprecious stones, were among the most important luxury goods during the Middle Preclassic Period. They were traded extensively along the routes that crisscrossed the entire Mesoamerican cultural area.

The settlement of San Lorenzo (Veracruz) was built in about 1150 BC on an artificially created plateau overlooking the coastal plains of the Gulf of Mexico. Mesoamerica's first large monumental city, it covered an area of more than 1700 acres (688 hectares) and was composed of earthen public and religious buildings, and monumental basalt sculptures.

From a political standpoint, San Lorenzo was the capital of a complex chiefdom whose sovereign lived in the monumental city and ruled over smaller monumental centers – governed in turn by noblemen – and numerous farm villages. The economic structure of the Olmec chiefdoms relied on farming the coastal floodplains, whose vast network of rivers, lagoons and marshes also offered abundant aquatic resources such as fish and shellfish. It is thought that the farmers paid a tribute – in the form of goods and labor – to the members of an elite class who were probably distinguished from the rest of the population by their supposedly noble ancestry. We have no knowledge of the elites' political and administrative divisions. Nevertheless, it is evident that they managed the city's political life and established relations with faraway regions, chiefly to trade luxury goods, and foster diplomatic and marital alliances. San Lorenzo's trade networks extended to western Chiapas – the Olmec imported iron minerals and goods such as

cocoa beans and amber – and the distant regions of Oaxaca and central Mexico, where artifacts reflecting Olmec artistic standards became widespread. It seems that in Soconusco, where the Mokaya culture had originally developed, San Lorenzo had a much more direct influence.

The presence of monumental sculptures (the only ones that existed at the time outside the urban area of San Lorenzo) suggests settlement by an elite class with direct ties to the capital city, probably through marital policies.

The fact that San Lorenzo's main trade and political relations involved Mixe-Zoquean-speaking areas such as western Chiapas and Soconusco implies that, even in this early period, the isthmus was effectively a linguistic, cultural and political *koiné* dominated by Olmec political powers.

Nevertheless, San Lorenzo was not the only Olmec chiefdom in the area around the Gulf of Mexico at the end of the 2nd millennium. Though our knowledge of the Olmec political structure of this period is still quite hazy, it is likely that other cities such as La Venta, Laguna de los Cerros and Tres Zapotes served as the capitals of their own political realms, which shared a similar political and economic structure, and a parallel set of beliefs.

The best evidence of this belief system comes from the sculptures that adorned the monumental center of San Lorenzo. The enormous monumental thrones – mistakenly referred to as "altars" – may be one of the clearest "political manifestos" of ancient Mesoamerica. Depicted on the front of the monument is a ruler seated at the edge of a cave, represented as the gaping maw of the Earth Monster. In some cases the ruler, who seems to have come from the bowels of the earth, holds a were-jaguar, the symbol of the supernatural powers of the underworld. The significance of the relief clearly alludes to a well-known Mesoamerican cosmological conception. The ruler is set in a cosmologically significant position, on the threshold between the world of men and the "Heart of the Mountain of Sustenance," the place that is dominated by water and fertility gods, and contains the "seeds" of men, animals and plants. The ruler is thus portrayed as the mediator of these forces, the one responsible for the well-being of the population and the productivity of their maize fields. But the thrones also tell us something else: these enormous basalt blocks, weighing tons and quarried miles away, were tangible proof of the managerial capacities of a lord who had successfully organized and fed the workmen required to move and carve these blocks.

In some cases, the thrones were then resculpted and transformed into colossal heads that were effectively the portraits of rulers.

Their monumental power is due not only to their enormous size, but also to their exquisite formal balance and stark, simple details. For the first time in the history of Mesoamerican art, these colossal heads give us the chance to see the somatic features of specific figures, i.e., the political leaders of those faraway lands. It is likely that the thrones were transformed into colossal heads following the king's death. It seems that his throne was thus turned into a funerary monument destined for a specific area of the center as a way of handing down the king's memory.

San Lorenzo was the chief Olmec city until 1000–900 BC (essentially the start of the Middle Preclassic Period, 900–300 BC), when for unknown reasons it lost its dominant role, triggering a crisis with enormous repercussions and a power vacuum that was quickly filled by other settlements.

30 - The Olmec thrones, mistakenly referred to as altars, were used as chairs by the rulers. "Altar" No. 5 from La Venta (Tabasco) is shown here. The thrones were decorated with motifs alluding to the mythological cycle of the Maize God and his connection with the local concept of royalty (Villahermosa Park Museum, Tabasco).

31 - Starting in 600 BC, bas-relief stelae spread throughout the Olmec area, gradually replacing freestanding sculptures. Monument 19 at La Venta portrays a ruler protected by a rattlesnake, probably his divine "patron" (Villahermosa Park Museum, Tabasco).

32-33 - THE MONUMENTAL CENTER OF LA VENTA (TABASCO) IS COMPOSED OF DOZENS OF BUILDINGS MADE OF RAMMED EARTH, AND IS DOMINATED BY THE IMPRESSIVE MAIN PYRAMID, EFFECTIVELY A REPLICA OF THE MOUNTAIN OF SUSTENANCE.

33 LEFT - A MONUMENTAL TOMB WAS DISCOVERED AT LA VENTA COMPLEX A, AND THE SMALL JADEITE FIGURINE WAS FOUND AMONG ITS LAVISH ACCOUTREMENTS (NATIONAL MUSEUM OF ANTHROPOLOGY, MEXICO CITY).

33 RIGHT - THE THRONE REFERRED TO AS ALTAR 4 AT LA VENTA PORTRAYS AN OLMEC RULER SEATED IN THE GAPING MAW OF THE EARTH MONSTER, WHOSE FACE IS VISIBLE ON THE UPPER PART (VILLAHERMOSA PARK MUSEUM, TABASCO).

In the urban area, the site of La Venta (Tabasco) rose as the head of a new and powerful chiefdom, and monuments like colossal heads and thrones closely resembling the ones from San Lorenzo were discovered here. Unlike San Lorenzo, La Venta was not reoccupied millennia later, and this has allowed us to get a better idea of its original architectural layout. The monumental center, composed of dozens of buildings made of rammed earth and finished with plaster, was laid out around a large central plaza.

Several structures overlooked the plaza, such as the enormous platform of the acropolis (which probably held architectural complexes used for public and political purposes) and the pyramid 100 ft (30.5 m) in height, effectively a replica of the Mountain of Sustenance also depicted in the reliefs on the monumental thrones discovered in the plaza.

The pyramid separated the main plaza from what has been named Complex A, a series of patios and buildings that probably represented the heart of the ritual space, symbolically associated with the underworld. The colossal heads — and, again, they probably represented dead kings — were found here, alongside royal burials and extensive evidence of ancient ritual practices. However, the most surprising discovery was the burial of numerous overlaid "pavements," made of tons of green serpentine or jadeite blocks, in some cases arranged to form geometric motifs that look like cosmograms. Here too, these items replicated a cosmological concept: the large deposits of greenstone buried at the foot of the pyramid represented the "fertile" underground water hidden inside the Mountain of Sustenance.

The celebration of similar rituals inside the monumental center was tied to a religious system that revolved around the circulation of the aquatic forces of fertility. At the same time, however, it was also connected to a political and ideological system whose legitimacy was based on controlling these forces. This interpretation would explain the growing symbolic association between the ruler and the Maize God: for example, ears of maize decorated the royal headdresses. The formalization of these systems, and their iconographic and symbolic expression in a vast complex of artwork, seem to have been the driving force of the Olmec culture, and the reason it became so widespread in Preclassic Mesoamerica.

During La Venta's heyday, axehead-like pieces of rock and small stone sculptures depicting supernatural beings tied to the underworld became common in most of Mesoamerica. The emerging elite of the various regions considered the ritual use of these objects a form of legitimization, sharing the symbolic system that had been formalized by the Olmec.

The spread of Olmec materials during La Venta's golden age (900–400 BC) does not necessarily mean that La Venta or other Olmec sites exercised direct authority over the other Mesoamerican regions. In fact, independent regional political entities were forming throughout Mesoamerica, and their ruling groups interacted in an extensive trade network, in which the Olmec style seems to have represented a lingua franca of power.

The importance of these relations – and of the diplomatic events and marriages that sealed them – seems to have triggered the profound change in Olmec monumental art evident after 700 BC, when enormous bas-relief stelae slowly began to replace the large freestanding sculptures common until then.

This can be seen not only at La Venta, but also at the emerging site of Tres Zapotes, which by 600 BC had become the most important Olmec center on the Gulf of Mexico. Notably, bas-relief stelae depicting the encounters of nobles, together with other signs of intense contacts with the Olmec world around the Gulf of Mexico, also began to appear in regions with which the Olmec were in close contact: the Pacific coast of Chiapas and Guatemala (the sites of Pijijiapan, Tzutzuculi and Takalik Abaj), the Central Depression (La Libertad) and western Chiapas (Chiapa de Corzo and San Isidro). It seems that the main relations continued to involve the Mixe-Zoquean language regions. Nevertheless, portable Olmec objects became far more widespread during this phase, reaching distant regions such as central Mexico, Guerrero and Oaxaca, where new political structures, which were destined to become extremely important, were starting to form.

34 - This ceremonial celt made of jadeite portrays an Olmec deity with the typical "flaming eyebrows," probably a manifestation of the newborn Maize God (British Museum, London).

35 - This fragment of an Olmec breastplate made of jadeite depicts a human face. The two glyphs engraved in the upper left part of the object indicate that it was reused by the Maya many centuries after it was carved (British Museum, London).

37 BOTTOM - THIS OLMEC CARVING, MADE OF TERRACOTTA, PORTRAYS A FIGURE WITH A COMPLEX HEADDRESS SET ON ITS MISSHAPEN SKULL. THE CHILDLIKE BODY PROBABLY ALLUDES TO THE POWERFUL SYMBOLIC SIGNIFICANCE OF CHILDREN (NATIONAL MUSEUM OF ANTHROPOLOGY, MEXICO CITY).

36 - THE MESOAMERICAN PRECLASSIC WAS A PERIOD OF GREAT CULTURAL DEVELOPMENT IN VARIOUS REGIONS. IMPORTANT SETTLEMENTS LIKE TLATILCO, THE PROVENANCE OF THIS CERAMIC HEAD, DEVELOPED IN THE MEXICAN BASIN (NATIONAL MUSEUM OF ANTHROPOLOGY, MEXICO CITY).

37 TOP - THIS OLMEC CARVING PORTRAYS A FIGURE WITH TYPICAL OLMEC FACIAL FEATURES. THESE FIGURINES WERE EXTREMELY COMMON THROUGHOUT MESOAMERICA IN THE PRECLASSIC PERIOD (NATIONAL MUSEUM OF ANTHROPOLOGY, MEXICO CITY).

38 - This terracotta sculpture portraying a figure in a contortionist pose is from the cemetery discovered at Tlatilco, in central Mexico (National Museum of Anthropology, Mexico City).

39 - The carving known as "The Wrestler" is one of the finest examples of the formal quality of Late Olmec sculpture (National Museum of Anthropology, Mexico City).

40 - THIS OLMEC MASK, MADE OF JADEITE MOSAIC, IS FROM THE GUERRERO REGION (PRIVATE COLLECTION).

41 - GREEN STONE WAS ASSOCIATED WITH WATER AND FERTILITY, FUNDAMENTAL CONCEPTS IN THE COSMOLOGY AND POLITICAL IDEOLOGY OF THE OLMEC (DENVER ART MUSEUM, USA).

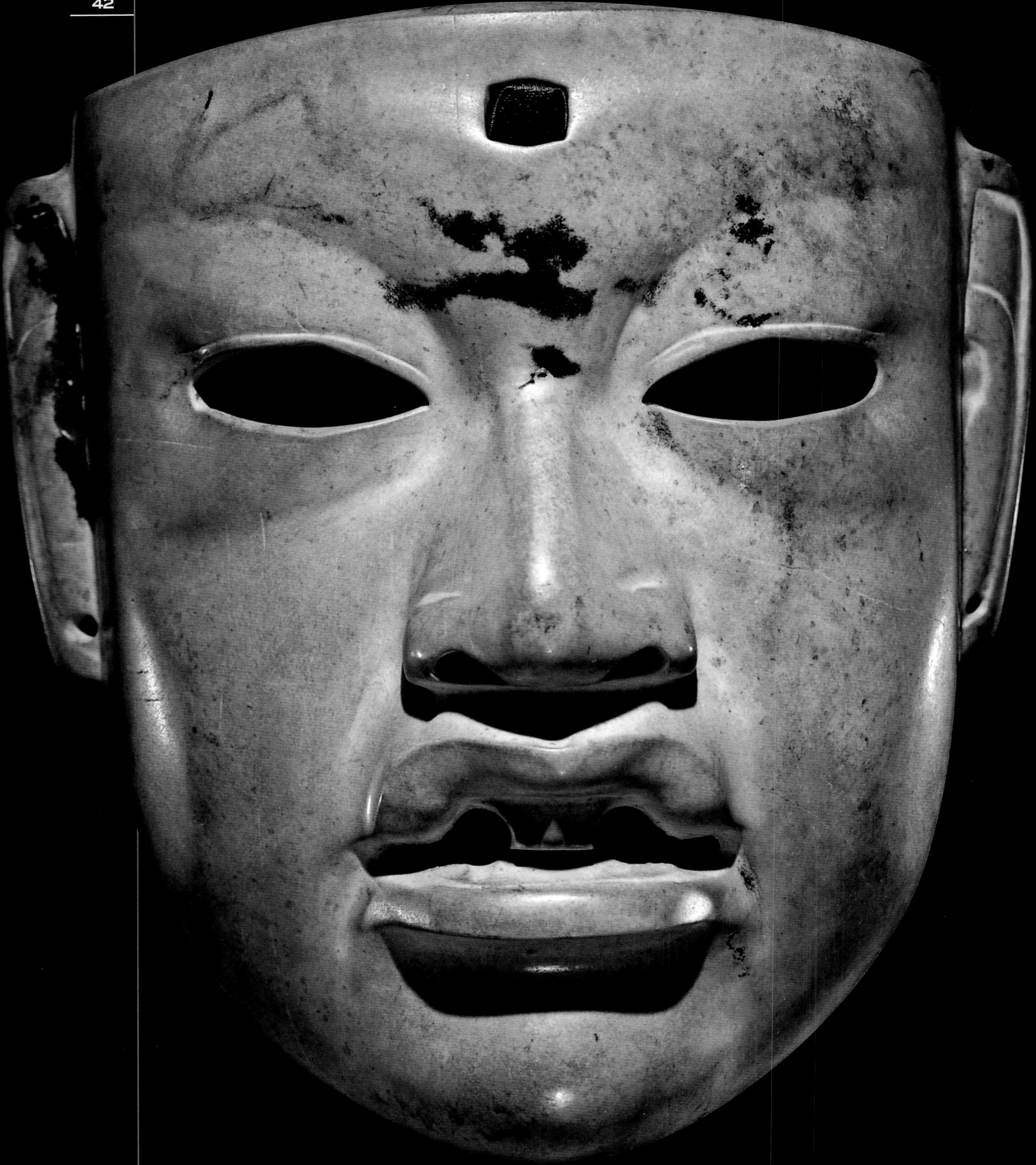

42 - This Olmec mask, carved from whitish jadeite, is from Río Pesquero (Veracruz) (private collection).

43 - This Olmec mask from Costa Rica portrays the typical Olmec were-jaguar (Denver Art Museum, USA).

THE BIRTH OF THE MAYA CIVILIZATION

44 - The city of Kaminaljuyú was one of the most important Preclassic Maya centers of the Guatemalan highlands, and an important site for the production of sculptures. Left, Stele 9, dated between 700 and 500 BC; right, Stele 11, dated between 200 and 1 BC, portraying a Maya ruler (National Museum of Archaeology, Guatemala City).

It is surprising how little is known about the origins of the lowland Maya civilization during the Olmec period and about the ancient relationships between these two cultures. During San Lorenzo's heyday, most of the Maya area was probably still occupied by groups of hunter-gatherers, and numerous farming villages began to flourish in the tropical lowlands of Guatemala and the Yucatán Peninsula after the fall of this important Olmec center. At the western edge of the lowlands, the sites of Seibal and Altar de Sacrificios were founded near the Usumacinta River and Río de la Pasión, possibly by Mixe-Zoque settlers. On the eastern side of the Yucatán Peninsula (in modern-day Belize) – one of the most culturally dynamic Maya areas during this period – villages like Cuello, Colhá, Barton Ramie, Nohmul and Cahal Pech were established. Centers that would later become important cities, such as Tikal, Uaxactún, Cival, San Bartolo, Río Azul, Nakbé and El Mirador, were established in the Petén area of Guatemala. The rapid development of the Maya culture during the Mamom phase (850–300 BC), chiefly by groups of settlers that spoke the Mayan-Cholan language, culminated in about 600 BC with the establishment of the region's first hierarchical societies, the most important of which were in the area of Tikal-Uaxactún and the Mirador Basin. El Mirador and Nakbé were founded in the latter area, possibly by settlers from Belize. Nakbé was the first center to be transformed into a great capital of the Mirador Basin. By 500 BC it already had a wealth of monumental stone buildings finished in plaster and stuccowork, and large bas-relief stelae decorated with images of nobles and kings.

During the same period, similar developments were taking place in the Guatemala highlands, where the village of Kaminaljuyú was founded in about 800 BC. The settlement enjoyed an architectural boom starting in about 600 BC, becoming the most important city of the Maya highlands.

The period between 600 and 300 BC was thus characterized by the rapid growth of important regional states in

45 - This Olmec sculpture is from Cruz del Milagro (Veracruz). Though it is known as "The Prince," it is likely that this work – like others of the same type – portrays a governor from a politically marginal center ruled by one of the great Olmec capitals (Xalapa Anthropology Museum, Veracruz).

the Maya area, and their initial development coincided with the height of the Olmec kingdom of La Venta. The role that the Olmec from La Venta and other isthmian settlements played in the birth of the first great Maya political entities is still unclear, given the fact that there is no solid evidence of direct contact between them. At the same time, however, it is unlikely that the lowland Maya kingdoms could have developed without any contact with the isthmus. It is possible that the two areas came into contact in the upper Grijalva Valley, where the important Zoque site of La Libertad was located, and along the western edge of the lowlands, where – as we have seen – Mixe-Zoque settlers founded centers such as Seibal and Altar de Sacrificios, which later became important Maya cities. The presence of Olmec iconographic elements on the ancient stelae at Nakbé seems to testify to the fact that there must have been contact, though its extent is still unclear to us.

Nevertheless, what is certain is that, in turn, the new political structures of the Maya lowlands upset the equilibrium of the Olmec world, quickly leading to the abandonment of La Venta and La Libertad in about 400 BC. These events seem to have triggered a crisis in the Mixe-Zoque world that, in the two centuries that followed, also affected Tres Zapotes (Veracruz), Chiapa de Corzo (Chiapas) and other cities in the upper Grijalva Valley.

The fall of La Venta marked the demise of the Olmec culture per se and ended the domination of the Gulf regions over much of Mesoamerica. Nevertheless, this did not mean that the Mixe-Zoque groups disappeared from the Mesoamerican political scene. In fact, in the centuries after 300 BC intense and documented interactions between the Maya and the Post-Olmec Mixe-Zoque populations led to the rise of cultural and political elements that would prove to be fundamental shaping forces in the centuries that followed.

2

THE RISE
OF REGIONAL TRADITIONS
(300 BC–AD 250)

As we have seen, in about 300 BC (the start of the Late Preclassic Period, 300 BC–AD 250), a great crisis – perhaps triggered by the Maya expansion from the Mirador Basin – struck the Mixe-Zoque world. In the Olmec area, La Venta had been abandoned a century before and Tres Zapotes was rapidly declining. In the Central Depression the Zoque abandoned the monumental center of La Libertad, pressured by Maya groups, whose proximity is also reflected in coeval objects from the Zoque site of Chiapa de Corzo in western Chiapas. For reasons that are still unclear, abandonment and destruction also occurred in the Guatemalan highlands between 300 and 200 BC, perhaps following conflicts with the expansionist lowland states. Indeed, there is no doubt about the fact that the Maya kingdom of the Mirador Basin was the most powerful political entity in the Southeast during this period. Important centers like Nakbé and Calakmul were also located here and came under the

authority of El Mirador, which became a capital in about 200 BC.

The public architecture of El Mirador took on colossal dimensions with the construction of one of the largest stone edifices ever erected in the Maya area. Moreover, it was constructed using large stone slabs set so that only the short end was visible, enormously increasing the number of hewn stones needed to build it. Evidently, the importance of managing public labor (also evident in the colossal structures of the Olmec) had become a critical mechanism for social control. This manpower was used to construct buildings that were organized based on cosmological models and served as backdrops for complex ceremonial activities. At the same time, the custom of large stelae with bas-relief carvings declined, probably due to the parallel spread of large buildings decorated with masks of deities, which became the hallmark of Maya architecture during this period.

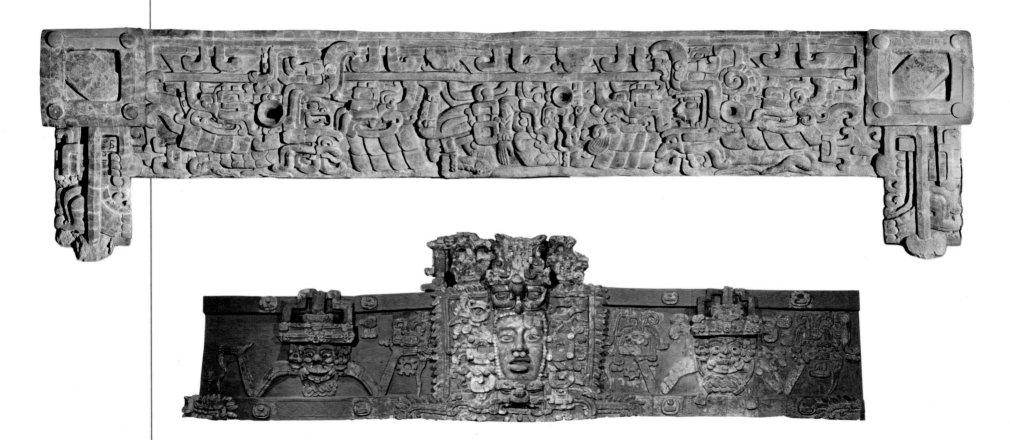

Archaeological findings indicate that the set of beliefs and concepts that later became the foundation of the Classic Maya religion already existed during the Preclassic Period. From a cosmological standpoint, the universe was conceived of as a series of overlapping levels: there were 13 heavenly levels and 9 underworld levels, and the Earth, inhabited by men, was in the middle. The levels of the cosmos were united by the large cosmic ceiba tree – the Great Mother – and the divine essences and "spirits" of powerful men like shamans and kings could transit through its trunk.

There were four *Pawahtun* or *Bacab*, depicted as elderly men, at the four corners of the cosmos. The combination between these figures and the central tree formed an "image" composed of four points, which were arranged like the corners of a square with a central point.

This was the quincunx, the most widespread cosmogram among the Maya, and it was depicted on various works of art.

The Maya deities were supernatural beings composed of a "subtle" and changeable essence. As a result, they could assume different forms and reveal themselves as countless hierophanies. This makes it extremely complicated to come up with a general description of what we could call – somewhat inappropriately – the Maya "pantheon."

THE MAYA RELIGION

HISTORY AND TREASURES OF AN ANCIENT CIVILIZATION

The chief celestial deity was Itzamnaj, portrayed as a dragon, who could also manifest himself through his "alter ego" in the form of a bird. Ahau-Kin, the Sun, also moved through the Upperworld: in the form of a jaguar-warrior, he would plunge into the Underworld at night and re-emerge victoriously the following morning. In its transit, the Sun was preceded by the planet Venus, its "elder twin" whose cycle was so important in Maya warfare. The two celestial bodies were also manifested as the divine twins of the *Popol Vuh*, the great epic cycle of the Maya: Hun Ajaw ("One Lord," Venus) and Yax B'alam ("First Jaguar," the Sun), the sons of the Maize God who descended to the realm of the dead to play ball with the underworld gods and re-emerged in an astral form, thus becoming the two prototypes of Maya royalty.

The Rain God was Chac, depicted with a long snake-like nose and often wielding an axe, which he used to strike the clouds. Though often considered a celestial god, he was also associated with the great "store of fertility" in the heart of the Mountain of Sustenance, and thus also with the numerous earth gods. The Earth was conceived of as a monster known as the Cauac Monster, in the form of a great crocodile named Itzam Cab Ayiin or as an enormous turtle carapace. The Maize God Hun Nal Ye was continuously "reborn" from the back of a turtle. One of his manifestations was the "Jester God" often seen on royal headdresses, confirming the constant association between royalty and the Maize God. Another god closely associated with royalty was K'awiil, the god of blood and royal semen, and the true dynastic patron deity. His distinctive serpentine leg was depicted on the scepters held by the Maya kings.

Among the numerous deities of the world of the dead, two of the most significant are Lord One Death, portrayed as a wizened old man, often smoking a cigar, and the skeleton god that is referred to in colonial texts as Ah Puch, "The Fleshless One."

52-53 - THE REPRESENTATION OF A FEATHERED SERPENT IS FROM THE YUCATEC CITY OF CHICHÉN ITZÁ. DESPITE THE FACT THAT THIS DEITY, WHICH ORIGINATED IN CENTRAL MEXICO, WAS ALSO PORTRAYED IN CLASSIC MAYA ART, IT DID NOT BECOME WIDESPREAD AMONG THE MAYA UNTIL THE POSTCLASSIC PERIOD (NATIONAL MUSEUM OF ANTHROPOLOGY, MEXICO CITY).

54 - This censer from the city of
Palenque portrays the sun god
Kin or Kinich Ahau, one of the main
Maya gods. He can be recognized by
the typical "curl" between his eyes and
his protruding tongue (National
Museum of Anthropology,
Mexico City).

55 - This marker from the ball court in
Toniná presents the figure of a
dignitary making an offering. The
ballgame was one of the most
important rituals associated with Maya
royalty, and with worship of the Sun
and Venus (National Museum of
Anthropology, Mexico City).

56 - The death mask portrays the face of a king. The fangs indicate that he is dead, as this motif alludes to the jaguar, an animal that represented the underworld (Fuerte de San Miguel Museum, Campeche).

57 - The censer from Mayapán depicts the Rain God Chac (National Museum of Anthropology, Mexico City).

NEW INTERACTIONS BETWEEN MAYA AND MIXE-ZOQUE

Perhaps driven by the powerful state of El Mirador, after 300 BC the small agricultural communities of other Maya regions also began to develop into complex political entities. The Yucatec Maya in the northern part of the peninsula were concentrated around sites like Edzná and Dzibichaltún. In Belize the city of Cerros became the capital of a regional kingdom, while the Cholan Maya of central Petén undertook extensive building work at sites like Cival, Tikal and Uaxactún, erecting public buildings decorated with masks closely resembling the ones from the northern areas. In a very short time, the Maya lowlands were dotted with new settlements, gradually forming a complex political scenario that was developing in the shadow of the first great expansionist states.

Nevertheless, the rise of the Maya kingdoms certainly did not mean the demise of the Olmec culture of the isthmian region. In the northern part of the Olmec urban area, for example, the site of Cerro de las Mesas (Veracruz) enjoyed a period of great prosperity starting in 400 BC. Alongside Chiapa de Corzo and Tres Zapotes, it became one of the most important areas of what is referred to as the Epi-Olmec culture, i.e., the new cultural configuration of the Post-Olmec Mixe-Zoque groups.

This new cultural phase, once interpreted as a moment of "decline" of the Olmec culture, is now viewed as an important period of cultural vitality that was also fueled by more intense contact with the increasingly dynamic world of the Maya. It is also possible that the fall of La Venta drove Mixe-Zoque groups toward the Usumacinta Basin, further encouraging interethnic contacts similar to the ones that must have been taking place in the upper Grijalva Valley and the transitional areas between the Pacific Coast and the Guatemalan highlands. Paradoxically, just as the Olmec culture was waning, these contacts helped introduced many of its elements to the Maya area. Recently discovered evidence of these contacts comes from the extraordinary murals at San Bartolo (Guatemala), dated about 100 BC. The extraordinary scene of the investiture of the Maize God reflects a pictorial style typical of the Maya, but the god's face is portrayed in the purest Olmec style. This was probably due to the importation of the ancient notions of Olmec royalty, and its association with the Maize God, to the Maya area.

Another example of the intense contacts between these two cultural spheres can be seen in the brief but magnificent efflorescence of the Mixe-Zoque site of Izapa, on the Chiapas coast. Between 300 BC and AD 50, this ceremonial center produced hundreds of extraordinary bas-relief stelae that seem to be the outcome of a blend of Olmec iconography with elements that would later become distinctive in the Maya culture. These elements may have been the outcome of contact between Izapa and the Maya groups living in the Kaminaljuyú area. In fact, toward the beginning of the Christian Era similar iconographic elements were extensively developed at Kaminaljuyú when the site became the capital of one of the most powerful highland Maya chiefdoms. Kaminaljuyú also established important relations linking it to other Maya centers along the nearby Pacific Coast, such as Takalik Abaj, Monte Alto, El Baúl and El Balsamo.

This new intermingling of relationships and trade – but possibly also conflict – spawned some of the most important cultural innovations of the era, first and foremost writing systems and various Mesoamerican calendars.

58 TOP - THIS CLOSE-UP OF THE PAINTINGS FROM SAN BARTOLO SHOWS A DEITY INVOLVED IN RITUAL BLOODLETTING: IN HIS RIGHT HAND, THE FIGURE HOLDS A LARGE TAPERED IMPLEMENT HE IS USING TO PIERCE HIS PENIS, WHICH SPURTS BLOOD.

58 BOTTOM - THIS CLOSE-UP OF THE PAINTINGS FROM SAN BARTOLO SHOWS ONE OF THE TWO MYTHICAL WOMEN ASSISTING IN THE INVESTITURE OF THE MAIZE GOD, WHO HAS JUST BEEN REBORN FROM THE EARTH. SIMILAR INVESTITURE CEREMONIES WERE PROBABLY ALSO PERFORMED BY THE MAYA KINGS.

59 - THE PAINTED ROOM FROM THE SITE OF SAN BARTOLO (GUATEMALA) CONTAINS A SPLENDID SERIES OF WORKS FROM THE 1ST CENTURY BC, ILLUSTRATING MYTHOLOGICAL SCENES ASSOCIATED WITH THE LIFE CYCLE OF THE MAIZE GOD.

60-61 - THIS GOD FROM THE MURALS AT SAN BARTOLO IS PART OF A GROUP OF FOUR, INVOLVED IN DIFFERENT ACTS OF MAKING AN OFFERING TO THE MAIZE GOD.

All Mesoamerican populations shared the use of two calendrical cycles. One was the 260-day sacred calendar. This unusual cycle was established according to the periods in which the planet Venus is visible and the duration of the rainy season. This calendar is exclusive to Mesoamerica and is not found anywhere else in the world. Its cycle was based on the combination of 20 day names (which are similar in the various Mesoamerican regions) and a sequence of 13 numbers, so that the same day-number pair is repeated every 260 days ($13 \times 20 = 260$). This calendar was used mainly for divination: soothsayers would use it for astrological considerations to determine if a date was lucky or unlucky, and the types of activities that could or could not be performed.

Instead, the other calendar cycle was the solar one, composed of 360 days with a sequence of 18 months, each lasting 20 days, plus 5 "ill-omened" days, thereby aligning the cal-

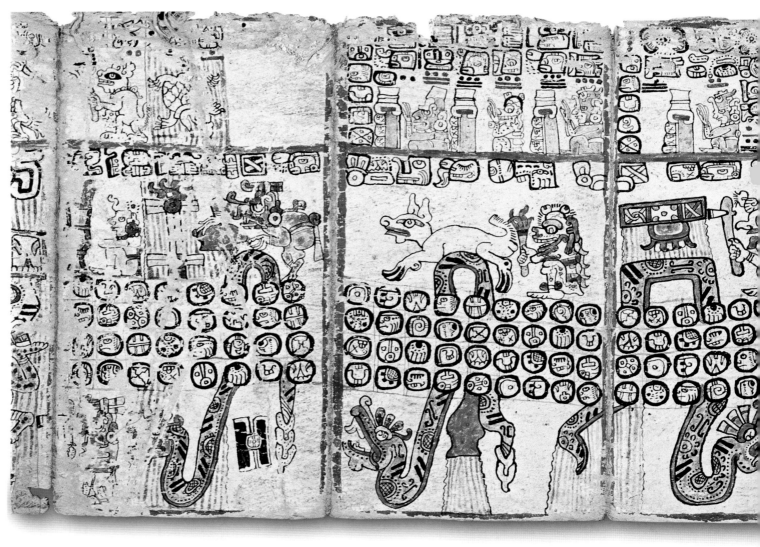

62-63 TOP - THE MADRID CODEX IS ONE OF THE FOUR MAYA CODICES THAT HAVE COME DOWN TO OUR OWN ERA. IN ADDITION TO WRITING ON MONUMENTS AND TERRACOTTA VASES, THE MAYA ALSO PRODUCED A LARGE NUMBER OF PAPER "BOOKS," MOST OF WHICH HAVE NOW BEEN LOST BECAUSE OF THE TROPICAL CLIMATE AND THE DESTRUCTION WROUGHT BY THE SPANISH CONQUISTADORS AND MISSIONARIES (MUSEUM OF THE AMERICAS, MADRID).

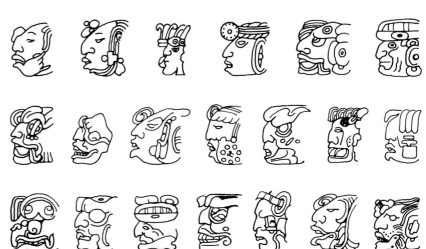

endar with the solar cycle. The solar calendar was used to mark the most important events of the year, the agricultural cycle and a long sequence of ceremonial celebrations.

The combination of the two cycles formed the Calendar Round, which was probably already in use during the earliest phases of the Olmec period and certainly by about the 6th century BC, not only along the Gulf of Mexico but also in regions such as the Oaxaca Valley. The combined use of the two cycles meant that each day was defined by double notation, using the following sequence: number (1–13) + day name according to the 260-day cycle + number (1–18) + month name according to the 360-day cycle. With this combination, a day would have the same sequence of numbers and names once every 52 years, a period that represented the Mesoamerican "century." This means that when we read a date on the Calendar Round, we cannot correlate it directly with a

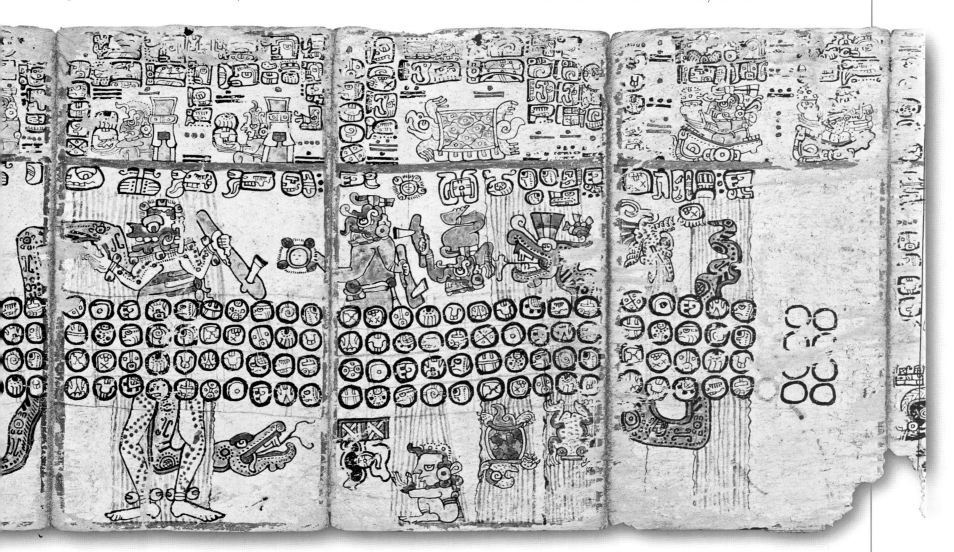

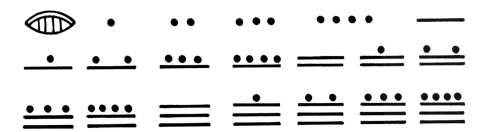

date on our modern calendar but only with a series of possible dates that are 52 years apart. In addition to these two basic cycles, there were also numerous accessory cycles, such as the one tied to the planet Venus and the one of the nine Lords of the Night. Evidently, the combination of so many elements in a single day, which according to the Mesoamerican mentality reflected the multiplicity of supernatural forces converging at a given moment, offered priests a more extensive range of action in their astrological and divination practices.

Another calendar system known as the Long Count developed in the isthmian area toward the beginning of the Christian Era, but it was shared only by Maya and Mixe-Zoque groups. This involved counting time starting with a mythical initial date corresponding to 3114 BC and associated with the creation of the universe. The number of days elapsed from that day on was calculated by combining a base-20 numerical system (which was actually modified slightly due to calendrical requirements) and a sequence of 5 periods of time that the Maya referred to as *kin* (1 day), *uinal* (20 days), *tun* (360 days), *katun* (7200 days) and *baktun* (144,000 days). In reality, this was also a cyclical system, because at the end of the 13th *baktun* the count would revert to zero. However, the fact that the 13th *baktun* has not ended yet (it will terminate on December 23, 2012) makes the cycle so long that it "appears" to be linear (the entire Pre-Hispanic Maya period is part of just one cycle). This has enabled direct correlation with the Gregorian calendar and allowed us to come up with a detailed reconstruction of the sequence of many events in Maya history.

The system of the Long Count was evidently invented by the Mixe-Zoque and appeared at the site of Chiapa de Corzo, where a stela with the date corresponding to December 9, 36 BC was discovered. Other stelae bearing dates ranging from 32 BC to the 2nd century AD come from various isthmian sites, such as Tres Zapotes (Veracruz), El Baúl and Takalik Abaj (Guatemala), and La Mojarra (Veracruz). The system was then adopted by the Maya in AD 292 and used until 909 to mark all the most important events in their history.

The Long Count envisaged the use of a vigesimal (base 20) positional number system that led the Mixe-Zoque and Maya to invent zero, an essential symbol in any positional system to indicate the completion of a position. In the Mixe-Zoque and Maya world, numbers were written using a combination of three symbols: the dot (denoting 1), the rod (denoting 5), and the flower or shell (denoting 0). Despite the

64 - STELE 50 FROM IZAPA CONTAINS ONE OF THE OLDEST REPRESENTATIONS OF THE DEATH GOD, PORTRAYED AS A SKELETON. IZAPA, ON THE WEST COAST OF CHIAPAS, WAS ONE OF THE MOST IMPORTANT RELIGIOUS CENTERS OF THE LATE PRECLASSIC PERIOD (NATIONAL MUSEUM OF ANTHROPOLOGY, MEXICO CITY).

65 - THIS SMALL WOODEN VASE IS FROM IZAPA. THE DECORATIVE MOTIF REPRESENTS A STRAW MAT, A SYMBOL THAT — THROUGHOUT MESOAMERICA — IS ASSOCIATED WITH THE RULER'S CHAIR, THUS MAKING IT AN IMPORTANT EMBLEM OF ROYALTY (PRIVATE COLLECTION).

excellent mathematical skills of Maya astronomers, which allowed them to calculate dates thousands of years in the past and future, it seems that this knowledge did not have any other practical or administrative applications. In fact, there is no proof of written calculations other than days and years in Pre-Hispanic Mesoamerica, although it also possible that such computations were written on perishable materials and thus have not survived.

In the isthmian area, the proliferation of small stelae decorated with bas-relief images of individual and deities, together with glyph inscriptions and dates from the Long Count calendrical system, coincided with renewed cultural vitality that seems to have radiated from the Zoque capital of Chiapa de Corzo. The city stopped using the "Maya styles" that had characterized its architecture and pottery in the centuries just before the Christian Era, developing new cultural models that eventually became typical of the entire Classic Zoque culture.

It is possible that this "renaissance" of the Zoque world, characterized by increased contact between the Gulf Coast, western Chiapas and the Pacific Coast, should be considered in relation to the concurrent crisis that struck many of the large political entities of the Maya. With the advent of the Christian Era, El Mirador gradually lost its dominant role and was finally abandoned completely between AD 100 and 200. A similar crisis swept through other important Maya cities such as Cerros, Nakbé, Cival and San Bartolo, and we cannot exclude the pos-

sibility that this may have been the result of growing conflicts among emerging kingdoms, paralleled by environmental deterioration. Despite the fact that even distant centers like Kaminaljuyú, the most powerful highland kingdom, also showed signs of decline at the same time, the crisis at the end of the Late Preclassic Period seems to have been concentrated above all in northern Petén, the area that was under the influence of the great kingdom of El Mirador. Instead, the crisis does not seem to have affected central Petén, where cities like Uaxactún and Tikal continued to develop, ultimately playing a key role in the renaissance of the Classic Maya culture.

The "collapse" of the Preclassic Maya culture of northern Petén was just the first of a long string of crises that characterized the next stage in Maya history. However, the Preclassic "collapse" was by no means an event that put an end to the cultural development of the Maya. It was an important transitional period in which the key aspects of the Preclassic culture were maintained: the ideology of sacred royalty based on the elaboration of older Olmec concepts, a political system based on the expansion and contraction of government entities organized around a capital that served as the administrative center, powerful political activities involving marital alliances, diplomatic contacts and wars, and the development of complex and diversified artistic traditions. All these elements would soon merge to become the hallmark of the extraordinary development of the Classic Maya civilization.

3

CLASSIC SPLENDOR
(AD 250–900/1000)

What is referred to as the Classic Period (AD 250–900/1000) coincides with the greatest cultural, political and artistic development of most of the Mesoamerican civilizations. For many years modern scholars considered the Classic Period an era of peace and prosperity, unlike the more warlike periods that followed. Today we know that this was not actually the case. Mesoamerican societies were always very aggressive and competitive, just like most ancient societies. In many cases, this competitiveness is what stimulated cultural and artistic progress, and Classic Maya society is an excellent example. The Classic Maya developed highly diverse artistic traditions that were nevertheless united by the fact that they shared a common symbolic language. This contrast between underlying cultural unity and the enormous variety of sculptural, architectural and pictorial expressions that may well be the most distinctive feature of Classic Maya art, which rivals the world's most important artistic traditions.

Nevertheless, a substantial difference can be noted between the Classic Period and the ones that followed, and it involves the ethnic-linguistic makeup of the main political

67 - THE DEATH MASK OF K'INICH JANAAB' PAKAL IS A JADEITE MOSAIC (NATIONAL MUSEUM OF ANTHROPOLOGY, MEXICO CITY).

68 - THIS ANTHROPOMORPHIC VASE, WHICH PROBABLY SERVED AS A CENSER, DEPICTS A SEATED MAN SHOWING HIS HANDS. FROM UAXACTÚN (GUATEMALA), IT DATES BACK TO THE EARLY CLASSIC PERIOD (NATIONAL MUSEUM OF ARCHAEOLOGY, GUATEMALA CITY).

entities. With the sole exception of Teotihuacán in faraway central Mexico, during the Classic Period political organization seemed relatively uniform from a linguistic standpoint, with groups like the Maya, the Mixe-Zoque and the Zapotec occupying different regions. Each one was distinguished by the creation of unique artistic styles and forms of expression, but there was a constant exchange of goods and ideas with nearby cultures. As we will see, the Postclassic situation, when large multiethnic regimes spread their influence over vast areas of Mesoamerica, was quite different.

For many years, scholars virtually ignored what happened in the isthmian area during the Classic Period, as they were convinced that the Mixe-Zoque civilization was eclipsed by the deeds of the nearby Maya. One of the reasons that undoubtedly contributed to underestimating the cultural importance of this region is purely geological. The lack of stone in the area adjoining the Gulf of Mexico meant that the great Mixe-Zoque centers were composed of monumental earthen structures, making them far less spectacular and "appealing" by modern tourism standards. However, this civilization has recently been re-evaluated. Important settle-

ments in what were once the Olmec urban areas, such as Tres Zapotes and Cerro de las Mesas, are now viewed as important centers of cultural development of the early Classic Period. This development evidently took place as part of the same Olmec-based cultural tradition, as demonstrated by the uninterrupted use of typical black pottery.

Due to the fact that it also served as the main route between central Mexico and the Maya area, the isthmus played a critical role. The chain of settlements extending along the Gulf Coast and into western Chiapas, splitting up into two branches (one through the Grijalva Valley and the other along the Pacific Coast), represented a primary trade route.

Tellingly, it was in this area that, toward the end of the Olmec era, important elements of the Classic culture developed, such as monumental stelae with bas-relief inscriptions, which represent one of the most distinctive features of Classic artistic production in much of Mesoamerica. The famous Stela 1 from La Mojarra (Veracruz), with its extremely long inscription and Long Count dates corresponding to AD 143 and 156, seems to be the direct antecedent of similar Maya monuments from later periods.

70-71 - EL TAJÍN (VERACRUZ) REACHED ITS ZENITH BETWEEN AD 800 AND 1000. THE PYRAMID OF THE NICHES, EL TAJÍN'S MOST FAMOUS MONUMENT, CAN BE SEEN ON THE LEFT.

69 - THIS TYPE OF TRIPOD VASE WITH QUADRANGULAR SUPPORTS CLEARLY REFLECTS THE INFLUENCE OF THE METROPOLIS OF TEOTIHUACÁN OVER THE MAYA AREA DURING THE EARLY CLASSIC PERIOD. A FUNERARY SCENE IS DEPICTED ON THIS VASE (BERLIN MUSEUM).

Significant cultural uniformity can be noted throughout the isthmian region, and it lasted until the end of the Early Classic Period (AD 600). During the first part of the Classic Period, the main contacts "outside" the Mixe-Zoque sphere no longer involved the Maya but the city of Teotihuacán, whose emissaries had to cross the isthmus to go to the Maya area where, as we will see, they played an important role in local political developments.

On the Gulf Coast, Cerro de las Mesas (Veracruz) was the main Mixe-Zoque center of the Early Classic Period, and

Corzo continued to be occupied for many centuries (as it is even today), becoming the main Zoque city outside the Gulf area. The site of El Mirador, along Río La Venta, probably became the local "hub" of Teotihuacán's trade and diplomatic network, which also extended along the west coast of Chiapas and Guatemala. Various settlements in the areas of Cerro Bernal (Chiapas) and Escuintla (Guatemala) seem to have formed a "chain" leading to Kaminaljuyú, the important Maya highlands center that established significant relations with the Mexican city during the Early Classic Period.

its significant production of stelae with bas-relief carvings, glyph inscriptions and calendar dates demonstrates that it was the capital of important dynastic governments. Along the rest of the Gulf Coast, a large number of settlements dotted with pyramids, which are now finally being studied more extensively, testify to significant population density and a cultural complexity that has yet to be understood fully. The site of Matacapan (Veracruz) probably had active contacts with Teotihuacán, as the Teotihuacán-style elements adopted in the architecture of the Veracuz settlement seem to indicate.

In western Chiapas, the ancient settlement of Chiapa de

The fall of Teotihuacán in AD 650 led to rebalanced political relations across Mesoamerica, and this isthmian area, which had had extensive contact with Teotihuacán, underwent profound changes. The Epi-Olmec styles typical of previous eras were almost completely abandoned. New forms of architecture and pottery rapidly spread throughout the area, which at this point was distinguished by the widespread use of highly sophisticated orange ware. New settlements were founded and ancient cities in ruins were reoccupied, such as the Olmec San Lorenzo. The sophistication of the artistic production that developed along the Gulf Coast starting in the Mid-Classic

Period is evident in the famous "smiling faces" from the Mix-tequilla region and the extraordinary group of terracotta sculptures unearthed at the site of El Zapotal. As far as stone sculptures are concerned, the series of "yokes," "axes" and "palms" that spread from the coast of Veracruz to various Mesoamerican regions is one of the most astonishing demonstrations of the skill of the sculptors from the Gulf Coast.

An important political entity ruled by El Tajín developed at the northern end of the Veracruz coastline during the Late Classic Period. Its monumental center is renowned for its

splendid structures, such as the famous Pyramid of the Niches and its numerous ball courts, many of which decorated with exquisite bas-reliefs. El Tajín reached its zenith at the end of the Classic Period, when the city was ruled by a figure known as 13 Rabbit, who was depicted on many of its monuments. The ethnic-linguistic identity of the constructors of El Tajín and other Classic centers around Veracruz was debated for years. Although this age-old problem has not been settled yet, it has now become clear that the Totonac, once considered the most likely candidates, did not arrive here until after the Classic Period. Therefore, it is far more plausible that El Tajín's initial

development should be attributed to Mixe-Zoque groups. It seems that the subsequent arrival of the Totonac must have contributed to the city's last moment of glory between AD 800 and 1000 – or to its final decline in about 1100.

In western Chiapas, also a traditionally Mixe-Zoque region, ancient settlements like El Mirador were abandoned and even Chiapa de Corzo seems to have undergone a period of crisis. A plethora of new settlements arose throughout this region as well, and recent explorations in the Selva El Ocote area have revealed the existence of a large number of monumental centers like El Tigre and El Higo. The surprising architectural sophistication of these sites is an excellent example of a period of great cultural development about which we still know very little.

Along the Pacific Coast, Santa Lucía Cotzumalhuapa (Guatemala) unquestionably represents the most significant cultural development of the Late Classic Period. During this period, Bilbao, El Baúl and El Castillo, which were probably the predominant centers in this region, produced numerous sculptures distinguished by an iconography that, in many respects, is reminiscent of the kind found in central Mexico. However, its numerous portrayals of ballplayers with yokes, axes and palms instead are a reference to coeval cultures from the Veracruz area.

Several authors are convinced that the culture of Santa Lucía Cotzumalhuapa is attributable to the early Pipil, a population that spoke Nahua (a language closely related to the one later spoken by the Aztec). They descended from central Mexico – although it is still unclear when this occurred – along the Gulf Coast, the isthmus and the Pacific Coast to reach the territories of modern-day Guatemala, El Salvador and Honduras.

What is certain, however, is that during this phase the regions of the Gulf Coast, western Chiapas and the Pacific Coast continued to maintain close relations, due to the fact that they were the main route of communication between central Mexico and Central America. The progress that is being made in studies on the isthmian cultural koiné of the Late Classic (AD 600–900) and Terminal Classic (AD 900–1100) promises to reveal many unexpected aspects of the Classic culture and offer better insight into the role that these groups played in the baffling collapse of the Classic Maya culture. We will examine the rise of this culture based largely on the information that is being revealed by the ongoing work to decode Maya writing.

WRITING

The origins of writing in Mesoamerica must be sought in the long formalization process of Olmec iconography. Starting in about 600 BC, its increasingly stylized symbols were transformed into standard symbols with coded meanings, thought they were still not used as writing per se. True inscriptions began to appear in about 300 BC and their "invention" has been claimed by various Mesoamerican populations. However, the advances being made in research show that inscriptions developed simultaneously in several regions: Mixe-Zoque (La Venta, Cerro de las Mesas, Tres Zapotes, La Mojarra), Zapotec (San José Mogote) and Maya (Kaminaljuyú, El Portón, San Bartolo, El Mirador). Thus, it would appear that intense contacts between these regions after the decline of the Olmec culture helped create the dynamic and extremely competitive cultural climate that ultimately led to the invention of writing. Given the essentially propagandistic nature of monumental inscriptions in Mesoamerica, it is clear that the adoption of glyphic writing – in other words, a system of public communication that made it possible to provide extremely detailed information – responded to political needs that arose after the fall of the great political entities of the Olmec. It is possible that this "narrative" requirement must be examined in relation to the acute competition existing among the new Post-Olmec chiefdoms. Each one struggled to assert itself in a chaotic and warlike political scenario in which every ruler needed to legitimize his power – no matter how limited – by recounting his feats.

Therefore, it is not surprising that the Classic Maya, possibly the most politically fragmented and competitive society in Mesoamerican history, brought glyphic writing to its highest expression, transforming it into a form of calligraphic art manifested on monumental sculptures, murals, codices and painted pottery.

Maya scribes were referred to as *ah ts'ib*, "scribe" or "painter" (interestingly, no distinction was made between the two activities), or *its'at*, meaning "artist" or "sage." The importance of scribes in Maya society is confirmed by the fact that these names often appear in the long royal titles of the kings.

Maya writing was based on the use of glyphs, or basic signs that were combined in quadrangular cartouches, which were normally paired in columns. There were various ways to convey meaning. Logographic glyphs pictorially represented the object to which they alluded – for example, the head of a jaguar was read as *b'alam*, "jaguar" – whereas phonetic glyphs instead corresponded to a syllable, regardless of its meaning. The combination of these two types of glyphs meant that Maya writing essentially worked like a rebus, in which the same word could be written logographically, phonetically, or using a combination of the two systems. Moreover, as in rebuses, the Maya would also use homonyms and similar wordplay.

Given the complexity of the Maya inscriptions, it is not surprising that it has taken years to decipher them. It was not until the 1950s that scholars like Tatiana Proskouriakoff, Yuri Knorosov, David Kelley, Floyd Lounsbury, Linda Schele and Peter Mathews started to understand how they worked, revolutionizing our ideas about the Maya culture. Before then, in fact, it was thought that the figures depicted on the stelae were peaceful priests and astronomers, and that the inscriptions referred mainly to astronomy and calendars. These pioneers in epigraphy instead revealed that the main characters portrayed on these monuments were rulers who recounted personal exploits, in which war played a leading role.

This revolutionary research has continued, and the recent work of epigraphists such as David Stuart, Stephen Houston, Simon Martin, Nikolai Grube and many others has allowed us to study the events of Maya history with the kind of detail and complexity that was unimaginable until just a few years ago.

72 - THIS JADEITE PIECE FROM THE EARLY CLASSIC PERIOD FEATURES AN ENGRAVED MAYA INSCRIPTION PAINTED WITH CINNABAR. THE GLYPHS ARE ARRANGED IN TWO COLUMNS, IN KEEPING WITH THE TYPICAL LAYOUT OF MAYA INSCRIPTIONS (PRIVATE COLLECTION).

73 - THIS CLOSE-UP OF A WOODEN LINTEL FROM TEMPLE IV IN TIKAL (GUATEMALA) SHOWS A PASSAGE FROM THE HISTORICAL INSCRIPTION SCULPTED BY THE RULER YIK'IN CHAN K'AWIIL IN AD 741 (MUSEUM FÜR VÖLKERKUNDE, BASEL).

74 TOP - THE FULL-FIGURE MAYA GLYPH IS A PICTOGRAPHIC REPRESENTATION OF ITZAM YÉ, THE ANIMAL MANIFESTATION OF ITZAMNAJ, THE MOST IMPORTANT MAYA DEITY. THIS MYTHICAL BEING HAS THE BODY OF A MACAW AND THE FACE OF AN OLD MAN, TYPICALLY USED TO REPRESENT THE SUPREME CELESTIAL DEITY (TONINÁ SITE MUSEUM).

74 BOTTOM - THE STUCCO GLYPH IS FROM A PANEL AT THE TEMPLO OLVIDADO IN PALENQUE (CHIAPAS). THESE GLYPHS FORMED LARGE PANELS WITH HISTORICAL INSCRIPTIONS (VILLAHERMOSA REGIONAL ANTHROPOLOGY MUSEUM, TABASCO).

75 top - This stucco glyph with a human face is from the Bat Group at Palenque (Chiapas) (Toniná Site Museum).

75 bottom left - The skeletal face of an underworld god is visible on the right side of this glyph from Toniná (Toniná Site Museum).

75 bottom right - This stucco glyph from Toniná (Chiapas) corresponds to the title of Divine Lord of the Jaguar of Venus, the name of a building in Toniná (Toniná Site Museum).

THE CLASSIC RENAISSANCE AND THE INITIAL EXPANSION OF THE TIKAL KINGDOM

After absorbing many Olmec cultural elements during the Preclassic Period and overcoming a crisis that led to the collapse of the important political entities of northern Petén, the Maya lowlands became the stage for the cultural development of dozens of city-states distinguished by their complex political life. The most important city in the first few centuries of the Classic Maya "renaissance" was Tikal (Guatemala). It is important to note that not only did Tikal survive the Late Preclassic Period unscathed, but that this crisis – and the ensuing collapse of the kingdom of El Mirador – may well have given it the political room it needed to expand. This does not mean that Tikal developed smoothly and uninterruptedly. Here too, the typical Preclassic artistic and architectural styles (most of which can be seen in the part of the city known as "Mundo Perdido") were abandoned, spawning the new Classic artistic style.

This spectacular city – whose unmistakable pyramids stand tall over the "sea" of the Petén rainforests – was created in the centuries that followed. From the earliest phases, the city's central plaza represented its monumental heart. The Central Acropolis, located on the south side, was the royal palace, and for centuries it served as the residence of the city's rulers. When the kings died they were buried in the majestic monuments built on the north side of the plaza, where the Northern Acropolis is located. The excavation of these complexes, and of those that were built nearby over the centuries, unearthed a large number of bas-relief stelae and other objects (often as part of funerary accoutrements) whose inscriptions have revealed the key events in the history of Tikal. As is the case with all other Maya cities, the stories we read in the monumental inscriptions were commissioned by the ruling classes for the purpose of propaganda. Thus, they only tell us about the extraordinary feats of these kings and reveal nothing about the life of the peasants who made up most of the population. In some cases, we must also doubt the truthfulness of the events that are recounted: a fitting approach with any type of propaganda. On the other hand, the very fact that we know dates, names and events is extraordinary in a world like that of Pre-Hispanic America, where much of ancient history is cloaked in daunting anonymity. Moreover, considering our knowledge of these ancient civilizations and their leaders, in some respects knowing what these rulers wanted to recount on their monuments is at least as important as discovering elusive "historical truths."

According to inscriptions found here, the fundamental event in the Classic development of Tikal, whose Maya name was Mutal ("Hair Bundle"), was the establishment of a new ruling dynasty by Yax Ehb' Xook ("First Step Shark") during the 3rd century. Unfortunately, there is very little information about him and his first successors. One of the most notable sources from this period is the famous Stela 29, erected when the city's second ruler Siyaj Chan K'awil ("K'awil Born in Sky") rose to the throne. The date on it (July 8, AD 292) represents the earliest documentation of the Long Count in the Maya area, and is the threshold conventionally adopted by scholars to mark the beginning of the Classic Period.

It seems that Tikal developed independently during the first few centuries of the new dynasty, and there are no signs of political relations with nearby domains. However, during the reign of Chak Tok Ich'aak ("Great Burning Claw"), who rose to the throne in the mid-4th century, something happened that changed the course of Tikal's history forever. The monuments narrate the "arrival" of a figure named Siyaj K'ak ("Fire is Born"), who may have been a military leader sent by "Spearthrower Owl," the lord of faraway Teotihuacán, the city that ruled central Mexico during this period. Significantly, the day of Siyaj K'ak's "arrival" (January 31, AD 378) coincided with the death of Chak Tok Ich'aak, who had probably been dethroned by the foreigner whose "arrival" thus seems to reflect nothing short of a military conquest. Under his leadership, in the years that followed Tikal extended its rule to a number of nearby settlements such as Uaxactún, Motul de San José and Bejucal, going as far as Río Azul. However, Siyaj K'ak never became the king of Tikal. In AD 379, shortly after his "arrival," Yax Nuun Ayiin ("First? Caiman"), who may have been a Teotihuacán nobleman, took over rulership of the city, inaugurating a period of direct intervention in Maya political events.

77 - This death mask was found in Burial 160 at Tikal, which held the body of a man who may have ruled over the city at the beginning of the 6th century AD. The mask is composed of pieces of green stone, shells and obsidian (National Museum of Archaeology, Guatemala City).

78 - THIS PICTURE SHOWS A MAYA NOBLEWOMAN AMONG THE LEADING FIGURES IN A COURTLY SCENE PAINTED ON A CYLINDRICAL VESSEL FROM THE LATE CLASSIC PERIOD. NOTE THE WOMAN'S FACE PAINTING AND THE REFINED FABRIC OF HER CLOTHING (NATIONAL MUSEUM OF ARCHAEOLOGY, GUATEMALA CITY).

79 - YIK'IN CHAN K'AWIIL, THE KING OF TIKAL, IS PORTRAYED IN TEOTIHUACÁN-STYLE WAR DRESS ON LINTEL 3 OF TEMPLE IV AT TIKAL. THE CHIN REST OF HIS HELMET IS CRAFTED IN THE SHAPE OF A JAWBONE (NATIONAL MUSEUM OF ARCHAEOLOGY, GUATEMALA CITY).

Probably to promote his acceptance by Tikal's nobility, Yax Nuun Ayiin married one or more women from noble Maya families, so that his descendants would serve as a link between the Teotihuacán authority and the city's dynastic tradition.

The famous Stela 31 at Tikal, erected during the reign of his son Siyaj Chan K'awiil II, is a magnificent expression of this synthesis.

The stela shows the new king, who rose to the throne in AD 411, dressed in a typical Maya style that seems to "mimic" the one of Stela 29. Alongside the ruler, however, there are two portraits of Yax Nuun Ayiin dressed as a Teotihuacán warrior, as if to recall that the new king (who was nevertheless unequivocally defined as the 16th successor of Yax Ehb' Xook) ruled under what was effectively the "sponsorship" of the city in central Mexico.

Under Siyaj Chan K'awiil II, who ruled until AD 457, the state of Tikal consolidated its predominance in central Petén through wars and diplomatic relations like the ones with Yaxchilán (Chiapas). In the latter, the ascent of Yoaat B'alam ("Penis Jaguar") to the throne in AD 359 sanctioned the foundation of the local ruling dynasty. Other important dynasties were founded under Siyaj Chan K'awiil II, probably through some connection with the events at Tikal.

At Copán (Honduras), for example, K'inich Yax K'uk' Mo' ("Great Sun First Quetzal Macaw"), who may have been a Tikal Maya of Teotihuacán descent, rose to the throne in AD 426, ushering in a period of powerful Teotihuacán influence in the city. When he rose to the throne, K'inich Yax K'uk' Mo' also presided over the coronation of Tok Casper, the dynastic founder of nearby Quiriguá (Guatemala).

A few years later – in 431 – at the other end of the Maya area K'uk' B'alam ("Quetzal-Jaguar") became the king of Palenque (Chiapas), where he is also cited on monuments as Siyaj Chan K'awiil II of Tikal.

We still do not have enough of the pieces of this complicated "political puzzle" to understand the exact scope of these distant events, but it is evident that through its relationship with the metropolis of Teotihuacán, Tikal managed to create an advantageous political structure in most of the Maya lowlands. Aside from the territory it controlled directly, Tikal also played an important role in founding a number of allied states. During this era, Teotihuacán influence – probably mediated by Tikal – extended beyond the boundaries of Petén to reach the northern areas of the Yucatán Peninsula.

Teotihuacán elements have been discovered at sites such as Becán and Dzibichaltún, whereas the city of Cobá, whose architecture evokes that of Petén, dominated the political scene of the east coast. Tikal also had an important ally in the Guatemalan highlands: Kaminaljuyú, a city that seems to have served as the link between the lowland Maya and faraway Teotihuacán.

Nevertheless, Tikal did not control all the lowlands during this period. A state called the Kaan ("Snake") ruled the northern part of Petén – the region of the ancient state of El Mirador – and was probably the direct heir of the city's ancient glory. It is not clear yet which city was the capital of Kaan in the early 5th century AD, but Calakmul (Campeche) is a likely candidate, given the fact that a few years later it clearly played a central role, and the city's muddled dynastic lists seem to indicate some sort of continuity with the ancient kingdom of El Mirador. To the east, in the area of modern-day Belize (which also saw great Preclassic prosperity), the site of Caracol was developing into the region's ruling city; its dynastic founder Te' K'ab Chaak ("Rain God Tree

Branch") rose to the throne in the early decades of the 5th century.

After reaching the apex of political domination in Petén, Tikal underwent a troublesome period that is still unclear, due to the fragmentary information provided by the monuments at this site. It is nevertheless certain that during the first half of the 6th century the city was toppled by a political crisis. The first inkling of this crisis can be seen in 511, when the six-year-old daughter of a previous king was crowned as the ruler of the city. More than 20 years later – in 537 – her brother Wak Chan K'awiil "arrived" at the city, presumably following a period in exile, and apparently managed to consolidate city power again. In 553, for example, he sponsored the ascent of Yajaw Te' K'inich II to the throne of Caracol, demonstrating that Tikal's political influence had also extended to the region of modern-day Belize. However, something in this new alliance evidently went wrong. Just three years later, the king of Tikal defeated one of the lords of Caracol in battle, testifying to the disintegration of relations between the two cities. In 546 Aj Wosal's ascent to the throne of the city of Naranjo, halfway between Tikal and Caracol, was not sponsored by the king of Tikal but by the ruler of Calakmul, the capital of the great northern state of Kaan, which was evidently extending its influence southwards.

Disaster struck in 562. A "star war" – a war commenced to coincide with a given position of the planet Venus – was waged against Tikal. Though it is unclear which city attacked Tikal, in all likelihood it was Calakmul, capital of the state of Kaan, acting in concert with Caracol, whose monuments portray Tikal's terrible defeat.

80 AND 81 - THE PYRAMID ON THE LEFT IS PART OF THE ARCHITECTURAL COMPLEX KNOWN AS MUNDO PERDIDO IN TIKAL. THE MUNDO PERDIDO COMPLEX WAS ONE OF TIKAL'S MOST IMPORTANT MONUMENTAL SECTORS DURING THE CITY'S EARLY DEVELOPMENT BETWEEN THE LATE PRECLASSIC AND THE EARLY CLASSIC. ON THE RIGHT, THE PEAK OF TEMPLE IV, THE TALLEST BUILDING IN TIKAL, IS VISIBLE IN THE BACKGROUND.

WAR IN THE CLASSIC MAYA CULTURE

Contrary to what has long been thought, war was a widespread activity in the Classic Maya world, where it was one of the main instruments of political conflict. There are dozens of depictions of battles and, above all, of prisoners who have been bound, tortured and humiliated by victorious rulers, shown trampling on them. The most famous Maya war images come from the Temple of the Murals at Bonampak, where in about AD 790 King Chan Muan II commissioned the fresco of a vivid battle scene and the events that followed, including the moment when the tortured prisoners are presented at the king's feet.

In the Maya writing system, there are numerous glyphs that allude to war and probably refer to different fighting tactics, although the differences are not clear yet: *ch'akaj* ("strike with

an axe") and *chukaj* ("capture") are some of the most common. There are also other verbal forms that refer to the seizure of banners or other symbols of power. However, the most important form of war was the "star war," which was indicated using a glyph representing a shower (of blood?) falling from Venus to Earth. The start of this type of war was established based on a specific position of Venus in the heavens (although we know of some cases of "cheating" on this coincidence). Apparently, these wars often concluded catastrophically for the vanquished populations, as in the famous defeat of Tikal in AD 562.

The fact that most of the information we have about ancient warfare come from inscriptions, which refer almost exclusively to the capture of noble prisoners, leads us to sur-

mise that in most cases these wars were waged by noblemen who followed some sort of code of chivalry. It seems that during the Classic Period there were very few cases of outright military conquest or annexation of the defeated state. At the end of these wars, the vanquished ruler was usually ousted and replaced by a new king, often from the same dynastic line. The new king formally became the victor's subject and in many cases was tied to him by imposed marital alliances.

Nevertheless, we should not underestimate the possibility that these wars also implied forms of sacking and destruction, above all during some of the more "tense" periods of Classic Maya history. One example of this comes from the region of Petexbatún, when a number of Maya settlements such as Dos Pilas were fortified toward the end of the Classic Period, point-

ing to a particularly belligerent political climate. A very recent discovery testifies to the disastrous effects of a military attack. Reservoirs that had been transformed into mass graves were found at the site of Cancuén, and they were filled with the dismembered remains of 43 people, including women and children. This discovery seems to demonstrate the progressive spread of more devastating warfare tactics, essentially anticipating what would happen in the Postclassic Period when large armies battled in out-and-out wars of conquest.

82-83 - THIS BATTLE SCENE IS FROM THE MURALS AT BONAMPAK (CHIAPAS). THE FIGURE ON THE RIGHT, WHO IS GRIPPING A PRISONER BY THE HAIR, IS CHAN MUAN II, THE CITY RULER WHO COMMISSIONED THE PAINTINGS AT THE END OF THE 8TH CENTURY.

The outcome of the Star War of AD·562 profoundly altered the political equilibrium of the Petén area. The royal lineage of Tikal was wiped out and the city experienced a long and difficult era – lasting over a century – during which no new monuments were built. The crisis faced by Tikal also seems to have been mirrored by the decline of some of its historic allies, such as Río Azul and Kaminaljuyú, whose power began to disintegrate in about AD 600. In the meantime, the state of Kaan, ruled by Sky Witness of Calakmul, rose as the region's new superpower.

Its leadership was consolidated by Sky Witness' successors, who started wars against Palenque (in AD 599 and 611) and continued to forge diplomatic relations with Caracol, sponsoring the ascent of various kings to the throne. When Naranjo tried to rebel against this new order, attacking Caracol in 631, the king of Calakmul waged a star war against the city that ended with the violent death of rebel king. By the mid-7th century most of Petén was ruled by Kaan and its allies.

Kaan reached its acme under Yuknoom Ch'en II, also known as Yuknoom the Great, who became king in 636. While he was in power, Calakmul was transformed into a splendid city full of enormous buildings, including the impressive Structure II, which had continuously been rebuilt since the Preclassic Period. The complex is currently part of an important and extensive excavation program. Most of the political activities of Yuknoom the Great, who commissioned 18 stelae during his reign, focused on maintaining control over central Petén, thwarting the attempts of Tikal-Mutal to rise again.

After Nuun Ujol Chaak rose to the throne, internal conflict broke out in the vanquished city. As a result, B'alaj Chan K'awiil, the pretender to the throne, was forced to withdraw to the region of Petexbatún in the southwestern lowlands. Under the protection of Yuknoom the Great of Calakmul, in 648 he founded a new Mutal here (now known as Dos Pilas), which must have been an enormous insult to the dignity of Tikal.

But Yuknoom the Great did not limit himself to sponsoring the creation of the dissident city of Dos Pilas. In 657 he declared another star war against Tikal, driving out the local king, who fled to Palenque under the protection of K'inich Janaab' Pakal, the only one of his allies who was flourishing during this period. In exile, the king of Tikal organized his counterattack, returning to Tikal and taking his revenge by capturing Dos Pilas, driving out B'alaj Chan K'awiil in 672. However, Nuun Ujol C'haak's reconquest was short-lived. Calakmul attacked him in 677, forcing him to leave the throne of Dos Pilas, and two years later he was defeated by B'alaj Chan K'awiil and Yuknoom the Great, whose alliance continued to be quite profitable. To seal this alliance, the king of Calakmul subsequently visited Dos Pilas twice, participating in a ritual dance in 682 to celebrate an important calendrical date.

Likewise, Naranjo was unable to escape the clutches of this powerful alliance. After attacking and defeating Caracol in a star war in 680, it was defeated in turn, probably by Caracol. Yuknoom the Great effectively controlled the political scene during this period, and on August 27, 682 he had Lady Six Sky, one of the daughters of B'alaj Chan K'awiil of Dos Pilas, marry a nobleman from Naranjo and assume leadership – albeit informally – of the rebel city, thus drawing it into the alliance.

Therefore, by the early 680s an alliance linking Dos Pilas, Naranjo, Caracol and Calakmul dominated the central lowlands, literally surrounding Tikal at the height of its crisis. Only the western territory were marginal to these events: this was the area along the course of the Usumacinta River and the adjacent regions, the site of kingdoms like Piedras Negras, Yaxchilán, Bonampak, Toniná and, above all, Palenque, the splendid city that had never broken its alliance with Tikal.

84 - MAYA WARRIORS WERE OFTEN NOBLEMEN AND THEIR CLOTHING INDICATED THIS STATUS. AN EXAMPLE CAN BE SEEN IN THE HEADDRESSES SHAPED LIKE SKULLS AND DEER HEADS WORN BY THESE BONAMPAK WARRIORS.

THE RISE OF CALAKMUL

HISTORY AND TREASURES OF AN ANCIENT CIVILIZATION

86 top - The enormous Structure II at Calakmul — nearly 150 feet high — is the outcome of many centuries of constant reconstruction. It clearly symbolizes the great power that the ancient capital of the kingdom of Kaan held over the Maya area.

86 bottom - This figurine from Jaina Island (Campeche) depicts a Maya noblewoman or goddess weaving using a backstrap loom (National Museum of Anthropology, Mexico City).

87 - This figurine from Jaina Island represents a Maya nobleman whose social status is evident from his large necklace, earrings and bracelet: only members of the nobility were allowed to wear such jewelry (National Museum of Anthropology, Mexico City).

88 - This death mask was found at Burial 1 in Structure VII at Calakmul (Campeche). These masks, made of green stone and shells (*Spondylus*), immortalized the ruler's face, giving him supernatural attributes (Fuerte de San Miguel Museum, Campeche).

89 - This figurine from Jaina Island portrays an old man emerging from flower petals, and seems to allude to a myth similar to the one of the Lacandon Maya, according to which the gods were born from flowers (National Museum of Anthropology, Mexico City).

Scholars have long debated about the type of political organization that must have distinguished what we refer to as Classic Maya "kingdoms." Some have interpreted them as small chiefdoms with an extremely simple structure, whereas other have tended to label these kingdoms as true states, whose extension and level of power were extremely variable.

Maya inscriptions tell us that each political entity was headed by an absolute ruler of divine origin, referred to as *ajaw* ("lord"), who governed with the help of a noble class divided into lineages or "houses" linked by kinship. Each *ajaw* ruled a political entity distinguished by a glyph-emblem composed of the name of the kingdom (which often did not coincide with the toponym indicating its capital) and a series of prefixes that would read *k'uhul ajaw...* ("Sacred lord of...").

In some cases the rulers, who would usually adopt long titles that included epithets such as "He of the 20 Prisoners," used different titles that have not been deciphered yet. One example is *kaloomté*, but its use was restricted to particularly important kingdoms and it thus seems to refer to some kind of superior dignity.

In effect, though each kingdom was ruled by an *ajaw*, not all *ajawob* (the plural of *ajaw*) were equal. As we have seen in several examples, sometimes the ruler of a powerful kingdom "sponsored" the ascent of the ruler of a smaller kingdom he controlled politically. The latter figure was often defined as *yajaw* ("His *ajaw*"), indicating the bond of vassalage that tied him to his "patron." The smaller settlements within a kingdom were ruled by local governors, who held the title of *sajal*.

Evidently, the hierarchical relationships that united the different settlements – and that were pompously displayed during various ceremonies – did not imply a parallel economic or administrative hierarchy. In most cases, each settlement was functionally independent and the various noble titles alluded more to a formal hierarchy than to actual administrative divisions.

As a result, this type of structure, which was maintained through a tangled network of formal deeds, wars, weddings and ambassadorships, was extremely weak and could fall apart at any time.

Severing the ties of subjection to one lord to move under the protection of an adversary lord did not entail breaking economic and administrative ties. As a result, this practice was quite simple and common. The abilities of a

particularly skilled ruler or a favorable set of circumstances could lead to the creation of a vast network of alliances and patronage relations that spawned veritable "superstates," as Tikal and Calakmul have been defined.

Nevertheless, these two cities are proof of the fleeting nature of these political entities, which could crumble in a matter of years.

The fact that political and ceremonial activities were concentrated at the monumental center, which served as the capital of the kingdom, also meant that control over the outlying area weakened as one moved farther away from the capital. Moreover, the boundaries of these kingdoms were not clearly defined by any means.

Because of these characteristics, the Maya kingdoms – which were subject to continuous cycles of alliances and rifts – have been dubbed "enormous political entities" in which the many "centers" were aggregated or dispersed in turn, based on specific political contingencies. This chronic "weakness" of the Maya kingdoms was nevertheless offset by the great strength of the system as a whole: this change-able and vibrant "galaxy" of *ajawob* ruled the Maya lowlands for over 1000 years, making it one of the most enduring political systems in the ancient world.

90 - THE AJAW RULED OVER NOBLES, FARMERS AND CRAFTSMEN.

91 LEFT - CATHERWOOD'S DRAWING REPRESENTS A PANEL FROM PALENQUE WITH THE KING JAGUAR SERPENT.

91 RIGHT - THIS FIGURINE FROM JAINA ISLAND (CAMPECHE) DEPICTS A RICHLY BEJEWELED AJAW ON A THRONE (NATIONAL MUSEUM OF ANTHROPOLOGY, MEXICO CITY).

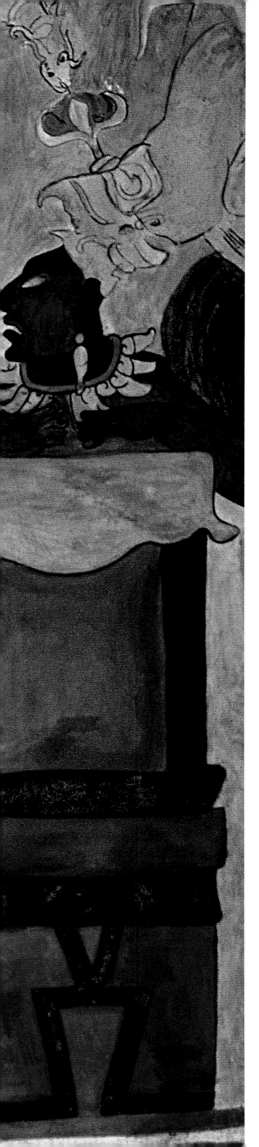

92-93 - THESE PARADING MUSICIANS WERE PAINTED ON A WALL AT THE TEMPLE OF THE MURALS AT BONAMPAK. THE THREE ARE PLAYING A TYPICAL MESOAMERICAN INSTRUMENT: A TORTOISE CARAPACE THAT WAS STRUCK WITH DEER ANTLERS.

93 - THESE MEMBERS OF BONAMPAK'S HIGHEST RANKS ARE LAVISHLY GARBED WITH HEADDRESSES AND ENORMOUS CAPES. THE BONAMPAK MURALS HAVE GIVEN US GREAT INSIGHT INTO THE CLOTHING WORN BY THE MAYA NOBILITY.

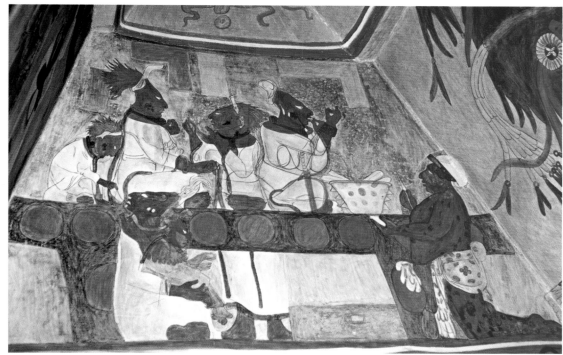

94-95 - THIS SCENE DEPICTS THE
INVESTITURE OF THE KING OF
BONAMPAK. NOTE THE JAGUAR-SKIN
SKIRT, SYMBOLIZING ROYALTY, AND THE
LARGE HEADDRESS WITH THE FACE OF A
DEITY FRAMED BY LONG QUETZAL
FEATHERS.

95 - THIS PAINTING FROM BONAMPAK
DEPICTS A GROUP OF NOBLEWOMEN
PRACTICING A BLOODLETTING RITUAL:
THEY ARE PULLING A CORD THROUGH A
HOLE PIERCED IN THEIR TONGUES. THE
WOMEN ARE SEATED ON A LARGE STONE
THRONE.

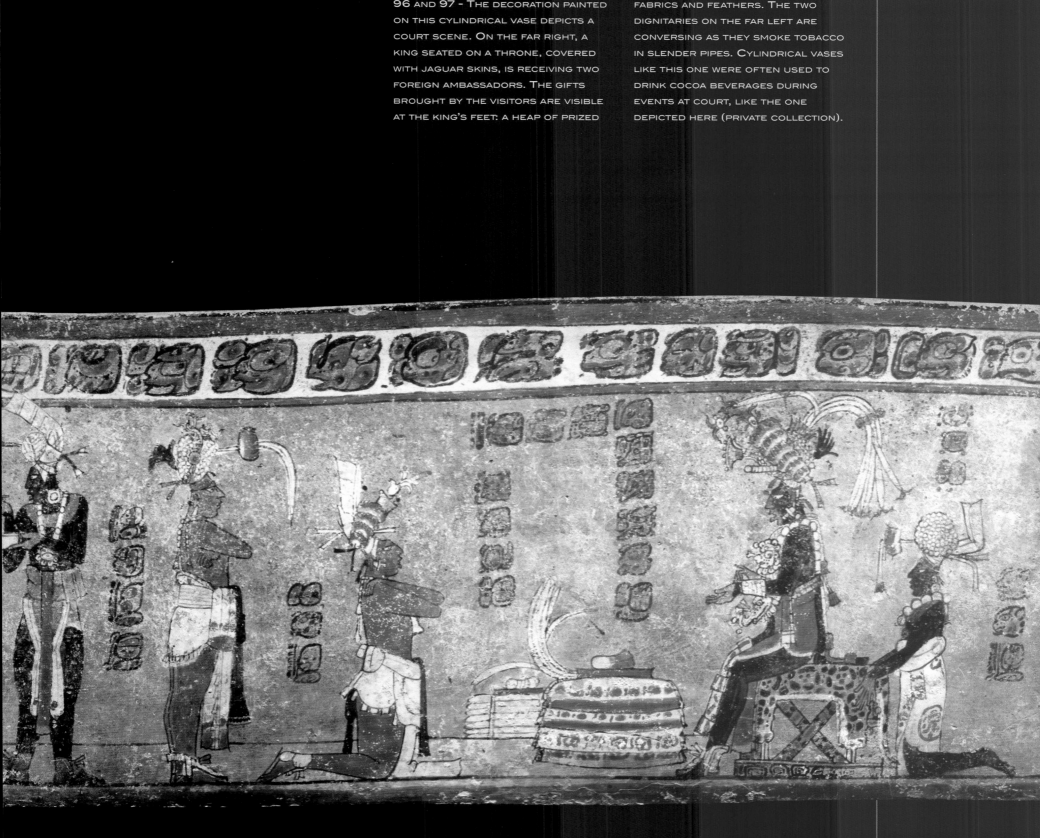

96 AND 97 - THE DECORATION PAINTED ON THIS CYLINDRICAL VASE DEPICTS A COURT SCENE. ON THE FAR RIGHT, A KING SEATED ON A THRONE, COVERED WITH JAGUAR SKINS, IS RECEIVING TWO FOREIGN AMBASSADORS. THE GIFTS BROUGHT BY THE VISITORS ARE VISIBLE AT THE KING'S FEET: A HEAP OF PRIZED FABRICS AND FEATHERS. THE TWO DIGNITARIES ON THE FAR LEFT ARE CONVERSING AS THEY SMOKE TOBACCO IN SLENDER PIPES. CYLINDRICAL VASES LIKE THIS ONE WERE OFTEN USED TO DRINK COCOA BEVERAGES DURING EVENTS AT COURT, LIKE THE ONE DEPICTED HERE (PRIVATE COLLECTION).

98 LEFT - A MAYA TRADER
IS DEPICTED IN A FIGURINE
FROM JAINA ISLAND. THE
FACT THAT THE MAN IS A
HIGH-RANKING TRADER IS
EVIDENT FROM THE FACT
THAT HE IS HOLDING A LARGE
FEATHERED FAN. THE FACIAL
DECORATION MAY DENOTE
SCARIFICATION (NATIONAL
MUSEUM OF
ANTHROPOLOGY, MEXICO
CITY).

98 RIGHT - THE FIGURINE
PORTRAYS AN OLD MAN,
PERHAPS DRUNK, WHO IS
HOLDING TWO CONTAINERS
WITH AN ALCOHOLIC
BEVERAGE. THE
REPRESENTATION OF
ELDERLY FIGURES IS VERY
COMMON IN THE
EXTRAORDINARY
PRODUCTION OF CLAY
WORKS FROM JAINA ISLAND
(NATIONAL MUSEUM OF
ANTHROPOLOGY, MEXICO
CITY).

99 LEFT - THIS NOBLEWOMAN FROM JAINA IS WEARING A GARMENT KNOWN AS A *HUIPIL*, AND THE SCARIFICATION ON HER FACE REPRESENTS BODY DECORATION (NATIONAL MUSEUM OF ANTHROPOLOGY, MEXICO CITY).

99 RIGHT - ONE OF THE LOVELIEST FIGURINES FROM JAINA ISLAND PORTRAYS A DIGNITARY DRESSED IN A "COAT" AND WEARING A HEADDRESS (NATIONAL MUSEUM OF ANTHROPOLOGY, MEXICO CITY).

100 left – This figurine from Jaina Island portrays a man dressed in a mysterious costume, probably war garb, and wearing a winged helmet (National Museum of Anthropology, Mexico City).

100 right – This noblewoman from Jaina is wearing a large pointed headdress. The figurines from Jaina were used as funerary offerings (National Museum of Anthropology, Mexico City).

101 left – A Jaina noblewoman is portrayed with a long *huipil* that leaves her shoulders bare (National Museum of Anthropology, Mexico City).

101 RIGHT - THIS FIGURINE FROM JAINA
ISLAND REPRESENTS A NOBLEWOMAN
WITH AN INTRICATE HEADDRESS
(NATIONAL MUSEUM OF
ANTHROPOLOGY, MEXICO CITY).

102 - This censer, used to burn copal, is modeled in the shape of a bejeweled noble figure donning a sumptuous headdress decorated with the heads of two feathered serpents (National Museum of Archaeology, Guatemala City).

103 - This censer is from the region of Lake Amatitlán (Guatemala). When incense was burned, the smoke would curl from the figure's open mouth (National Museum of Archaeology, Guatemala City).

PALENQUE UNDER PAKAL THE GREAT

As we have already mentioned, the kingdom of Palenque was founded in AD 431 by K'uk' B'alam I ("Quetzal-Jaguar") during the wave of new dynasties established following Teotihuacán's "entry" into Tikal territory, and it gradually became one of the leading powers of the western lowlands. In these regions Palenque had had to compete above all with Piedras Negras, a powerful kingdom on the east bank of the Usumacinta and also a rival of nearby Yaxchilán. Palenque was defeated by Calakmul at the end of the 6th century and then again in 611, generating a period of turmoil in the city that led to the rule of Lady Sak K'uk' ("Resplendent Quetzal") the following year, though she did not formally ascend to the throne.

Lady Sak K'uk remained in power until 615, when her

104-105 - THE ROYAL
PALACE OF PALENQUE,
WHERE THE KING HELD
COURT, IS VISIBLE IN THE
FOREGROUND, WHEREAS
THE TEMPLE OF
INSCRIPTIONS IS ON
THE RIGHT. THE CROSS
GROUP STANDS OUT
IN THE BACKGROUND.

105 - THIS MODELED
STUCCO FACE PORTRAYS
K'INICH K'AN B'ALAM, THE
SON OF PAKAL AND HIS
SUCCESSOR TO THE THRONE.
BECAUSE OF ITS
EXTRAORDINARY EXPRESSIVE
QUALITY, THIS PORTRAIT IS
CONSIDERED A MASTERPIECE
OF CLASSIC MAYA ART.

man was captured by the king of the enemy city.

During his long reign Pakal remodeled important city buildings, notably the enormous Royal Palace that was the seat of government. Religious and political ceremonies were held here, but it was also the royal residence. Tablets and bas-reliefs from the palace, which still dominates the city's splendid plaza, recount some of key events in the king's life, from his coronation to the capture of several noblemen from minor settlements that were part of the nearby kingdom of Pomoná. They also evoke the hospitality he extended to a noble from Yaxchilán and to Nuun Ujol C'haak during his forced exile from Tikal. This event and the previous war against Piedras Negras indicate that Palenque did not stay entirely out of the conflicts that pitted the superpowers of Petén against each other. These conflicts were also mirrored in the western regions, as also demonstrated by the fact that in the mid-7th century Piedras Negras managed to overpower nearby Yaxchilán with Calakmul's support.

twelve-year-old son became king, with the name K'inich Janaab' Pakal ("Great Sun? Shield"). Little is known about the early years of his reign, and it is likely that his influential mother continued to hold royal power for a number of years. What is certain, however, is that the conflict with Piedras Negras for regional sovereignty had never ceased, as demonstrated by the fact that in 628 a Palenque noble-

106 - K'INICH JANAAB' PAKAL WAS BURIED IN THE TEMPLE OF INSCRIPTIONS.

107 LEFT - THE KING'S SARCOPHAGUS AND ITS BAS-RELIEF LID ARE INSIDE PAKAL'S CRYPT, WHICH IS DECORATED WITH STUCCO BAS-RELIEFS.

107 RIGHT - THE BAS-RELIEF DECORATING THE SLAB OVER PAKAL'S SARCOPHAGUS PORTRAYS THE KING DRESSED LIKE THE MAIZE GOD, REEMERGING FROM THE MOUTH OF THE EARTH MONSTER AFTER DEATH. THUS, THE KING WAS ALSO REBORN THIS WAY.

108 - SOME OF THE MOST EXQUISITE BAS-RELIEFS IN THE MAYA AREA HAVE BEEN FOUND AT PALENQUE.

109 - THIS STUCCO HEAD FOUND UNDER THE SARCOPHAGUS REPRESENTS PAKAL (NATIONAL MUSEUM OF ANTHROPOLOGY, MEXICO CITY).

The reign of Pakal, who died in 683 at the age of 80, spanned more than 60 years, but it was not marked by wars like those of the other rulers of the era. Pakal evidently allowed the city of Palenque to prosper in a relative state of peace, thanks to trade with the Usumacinta area and probably also the coast of the Gulf of Mexico. As the end of his life drew near, the old king also began to prepare for his afterlife, building what has become the most famous funerary monument of the Maya world: the Temple of Inscriptions.

The Temple of Inscriptions, erected near the Royal Palace, is a pyramid with nine steps, alluding to the nine levels of the underworld. The pyramid is topped by a temple whose pillars are decorated with bas-relief stuccowork depicting the presentation of Pakal's heir K'an B'alam ("Snake Jaguar") by some of the king's deified ancestors. Several noble figures depicted on the balustrades of the staircase wear breastplates in the form of dates that allude to important events in Pakal's life, including the time he hosted the exiled king of Tikal.

Inside the temple, three glyph panels depict the entire dynastic history of the city, from its legendary origins (going back thousands of years) to Pakal's death, the ascent to the throne of his son Snake Jaguar, and future events up to the year AD 4772. The last six glyphs of the inscription read: "Great Sun Snake Jaguar, sacred Lord of Palenque, took care of the House of the Nine Images, the sacred name of the tomb of the Great Sun Shield, sacred lord of Palenque." In the floor of the temple, there is an opening that leads to a staircase descending to the base of the structure, which houses the great king's crypt (it may be been created inside an older building). The bodies of five or six men who had been sacrificed were found in front of the door to the crypt. The walls of the crypt bear portraits of Pakal's nine predecessors on the throne of the city, who seem to protect the large sarcophagus in the middle. The ancestors of the dead king are portrayed on the sides of the sarcophagus, whereas the lid bears the famous bas-relief representing Pakal at the moment of his resurrection from the world of the dead in the form of the Maize God. This ancient association – which, as we have seen, originated with the Olmec – is repeated in the inscription that runs along the edge of the lid and starts with the words "They closed the lid, the sarcophagus of the Maize God Pakal." The old king rested inside the sarcophagus together with an astonishing array of jade jewelry. The most important item is a death mask that has recently been restored to its original magnificence: on it, the artists of Palenque immortalized the image of their king.

In the early 680s, when Calakmul and its allies dominated the political panorama of the Petén area, a chain of events set off an important change that mainly affected the cities with ties to Tikal. When Pakal died (AD 683) Palenque was at the height of its splendor. Itzamnaaj B'alam II, a king destined for a glorious future, rose to the throne in Yaxchilán in 681. Most importantly, however, on May 3, 682 Jasaw Chan K'awiil I ("K'awiil that Cleans? the Sky"), son of the hapless Nuun Ujol Chaak, was crowned king at Tikal.

The first important event in the life of the new king is depicted by one of the splendid wooden lintels that decorated Temple I. The text, which was associated with an image of the three in triumph, tells us that in a battle waged on August 5, 695 Jasaw Chan K'awiil defeated none other than Yuknoom Yich'aak K'ak, the Calakmul king who had succeeded Yuknoom the Great. Thus, 130 years after the terrible defeat of 562, Jasaw Chan K'awiil I had finally managed to overturn the political balance of Petén once more, and through this victory he led Tikal into a new cycle of splendor. Another lintel from the same temple also sheds light on the ideological and propagandistic context in which Jasaw Chan K'awiil wanted to record his success. The king is depicted in the garb of a Teotihuacán warrior (although this distant city had already been torched and had long lost most of its power), and this theme is appropriate for the day chosen to celebrate this triumph: September 14, 695 – exactly 13 *katunob* (13 × 20 = 260 years) after the death of Spearthrower Owl, the Teotihuacán lord who had "sponsored" his city's entrance into Tikal. In essence, Jasaw Chan K'awiil came to Tikal as the one who would restore the former magnificence of the 5th century. Tellingly, he had an enormous pyramid built directly over the tomb of Siyaj Chan K'awiil II, the very king who had made that period of splendor possible.

Although the territory governed directly by Tikal when Jasaw Chan K'awiil was in power was never very large, during his long reign the city enjoyed a period of prosperity, and this was reflected in the imposing architectural programs that changed its appearance. In addition to the pyramid over the tomb of Siyaj Chan K'awiil II in the North Acropolis, the king also had two other tall pyramids built on the main plaza (Temple I and Temple II). He also had three complexes of twin pyramids built to celebrate the important endings of calendrical cycles in 692, 711 and 731. When he died in 734, Jasaw Chan K'awiil was buried inside

Temple I with impressive furnishings that included jade, shells, pearls, mirrors, jaguar skins, painted pottery and carved bone.

This array of riches was certainly well-deserved: the great king, who had risen to the throne during a period of crisis, elevated Tikal to renewed splendor. It was then up to his son Yik'in Chan K'awiil to transform Tikal's new dynamism into effective political sovereignty. Through a series of military campaigns, he again defeated Calakmul, which had plunged into an unending crisis along with sev-

eral of its allies, such as Yaxá, El Perú and Naranjo. Thus, he reconsolidated territorial control, which Tikal firmly maintained until the end of the 8th century, when a new crisis struck this great power. Information about this city is increasingly scarce during the 9th century, and the last stela was erected there in 869, the year that marked the end of Tikal's epigraphic records. This time, however, no one was waiting in the wings to take advantage of Tikal's demise. The last monumental citation of Kaan dates to just 40 years later: it was carved in stone in AD 909.

110-111 - THE BUILDINGS AT TIKAL STAND TALL OVER THE PETÉN RAINFORESTS IN GUATEMALA.

112 - THIS CLOSE-UP OF STELA 31 FROM TIKAL SHOWS THE FACE OF THE SUN GOD ON THE YOKE OF THE RULER SIYAJ CHAN K'AWIIL (TIKAL MUSEUM, GUATEMALA).

112-113 AND 113 TOP - TEMPLE I AT TIKAL DOMINATES THE MAIN PLAZA OF THE CITY, WHICH WAS THE HUB OF MAYA POLITICAL LIFE FOR 1000 YEARS.

113 BOTTOM - FOR CENTURIES, THE CITY'S KINGS WERE BURIED IN THE NORTHERN ACROPOLIS, WHICH EXTENDS ALONG THE NORTH SIDE OF THE PLAZA.

Jasaw Chan K'awiil's reign at Tikal also coincided with a period of renewed splendor and significant political influence for some of the cities of the western lowlands.

As we know, when Pakal died his son K'inich K'an B'alam ("Great Sun Snake Jaguar") became king of Palenque. In AD 687, just three years after his ascent to the throne, the new king won a major victory over nearby Toniná, a city whose political influence had grown in previous years through a string of military conquests of smaller neighboring kingdoms. After consolidating political control over the region, K'inich K'an B'alam undertook an architectural project that was even more ambitious than his father's, and its results can still be admired today in what is known as the Cross Group.

The main building of the new architectural complex is the Temple of the Cross, an enormous pyramid with 13 steps (mirroring the 13 levels of heaven). In the temple on top, a bas-relief panel portrays the dead king Pakal and his son, who are depicted next to a cosmic tree.

At the nearby Temple of the Foliated Cross, Pakal and his son are represented next to a maize plant. Lastly, at the Temple of the Sun the duo is shown at the sides of a shield, with the face of the sun set in front of two crossed lances. The three temples evidently represent three different aspects of royalty: the heavenly one, "fertility" and war. In all 3, other glyph panels summarize the city's dynastic history and illustrate some of the ceremonies in which K'an B'alam played a central role during the long coronation process.

After his image was immortalized on some of the most impressive Palenque monuments, K'inich K'an B'alam died on February 16, 702. The throne was inherited by his brother K'inich K'an Joy Chitam II ("Great Sun Precious Tied Peccary"), who undertook other important architectural programs. However, the disgrace of defeat was in store for him: in 711 Palenque was attacked by warriors from Toniná and the unfortunate king, whose fate is unknown to us, was taken prisoner and led to the victorious city.

And yet, defeat did not halt Palenque's development. Archaeological research conducted recently in the area south of the Cross Group has uncovered a series of refined monuments that date to the reign of his successor K'inich Ahkal Mo' Naab' III ("Great Sun Turtle Macaw Lake"), who rose to the throne in 721. Under him, there

114 - The monumental Temple of the Sun is one of the unmistakable buildings in the Cross Group, which was built by K'an B'alam immediately after the death of his famous father, Pakal.

114-115 - The Cross Group stands out in this fascinating overall view: the Temple of the Cross, the main building in the complex, is on the left; the Temple of the Foliated Cross is visible in the background.

were many military victories against the satellite kingdoms of Piedras Negras and other unknown sites. Chak Suutz' ("Red Bat"), who led the Palenque forces into battle, enjoyed great honor and was depicted on many monuments from the era.

Three other figures ruled Palenque – the last of whom at the end of the 8th century – and their refined monuments seem to indicate a relatively prosperous period. We also know that toward the middle of the century a Palenque princess, Lady Chak Nik Ye' Xook, was sent to Copán in marriage, and her son would later become an important king of this Honduran city. Nonetheless, there were also signs of impending crisis: the mention of another defeat at the hands of Toniná, coupled with increasingly meager and vague monumental records, marked the prelude to the sudden disaster that befell Palenque. All monumental activity came to a halt at the beginning of the 9th century and the city was abandoned forever.

THE LAST PERIOD OF SPLENDOR AT PALENQUE AND TONINÁ

HISTORY AND TREASURES OF AN ANCIENT CIVILIZATION

The troubles and collapse of Palenque effectively seem to have left a power vacuum that was filled by its rivals. During the 8th century Toniná achieved a series of important military victories that allowed it to dominate Bonampak and the Selva Lacandona region. Although little is known about the last phases of the kingdom, the fact that the city continued to produce monumental art longer than its neighboring kingdoms is significant. In fact, Monument 101 at Toniná bears the date of January 15, 909, the last Long Count date in Mesoamerica.

116-117 - THE MONUMENTAL CENTER OF TONINÁ (CHIAPAS) WAS BUILT AS AN "ARTIFICIAL MOUNTAIN" BY REMODELING A HILLSIDE WITH A SERIES OF TERRACES ON WHICH LARGE STONE BUILDINGS WERE ERECTED.

117 - THE MURAL OF THE FOUR ERAS IS ONE OF THE MOST MAGNIFICENT STUCCO BAS-RELIEFS OF THE MAYA WORLD. IN THE PHOTOGRAPH, THE DEATH GOD IS HOLDING A DECAPITATED HEAD; OTHER DECAPITATED HEADS ARE ON THE "KNOTS" OF THE BANDS OF FEATHERS THAT DIVIDE THE SCENE.

118 LEFT - THE STELA PORTRAYS ZOTS CHOJ, ONE OF THE SIGNIFICANT RULERS IN THE TONINÁ DYNASTY. IN THIS WORK FROM AD 577 HE IS DEPICTED IN A FREESTANDING SCULPTURE TYPICAL OF THIS CITY (TONINÁ SITE MUSEUM).

118 RIGHT - THE KING OF TONINÁ IS ARMED WITH WHAT LOOKS LIKE A LONG FLINT OR OBSIDIAN KNIFE, AND IS FLANKED BY AN INSCRIPTION. THE FIGURE BEARS THE FACE OF K'AWIIL, THE SYMBOL OF ROYALTY, ON HIS FOREHEAD (TONINÁ SITE MUSEUM).

119 - THIS SCULPTURE DEPICTS THE CAPTIVE KING YAX AHK' (GREEN TURTLE), FROM THE CITY OF ANAAY TE', WHO IS BOUND AND DRESSED AS THE DYING SUN BEFORE BEING SACRIFICED AT TONINÁ. HIS NOBLE TITLE IS INSCRIBED ON HIS THIGH (TONINÁ SITE MUSEUM).

120 - This bound prisoner is about to be sacrificed, as indicated by the long cotton earrings and the headdress typically worn by captives who were to be sacrificed. Stucco images like this decorated the walls of the Temple of War (Toniná Site Museum).

121 - K'inich K'an Joy Chitam II, the second son of Pakal of Palenque, is portrayed as a prisoner on a monument in Toniná after he was captured during a battle that was waged in AD 711 (National Museum of Anthropology, Mexico City).

122 top - THE REMAINS OF A MASK ARE CONCEALED BY THE VEGETATION THAT COVERS MOST OF THE SITE OF PIEDRAS NEGRAS IN GUATEMALA.

122 bottom - THE PRESENTATION OF THE HEIR TO THE THRONE IS DEPICTED ON LINTEL 3 AT PIEDRAS NEGRAS (PEABODY MUSEUM, HARVARD).

123 - THE BACK OF THIS THRONE FROM PIEDRAS NEGRAS BEARS PORTRAITS OF THE KING'S PARENTS, WHEREAS THE GLYPHS CONTAIN HISTORICAL INFORMATION (NATIONAL MUSEUM OF ARCHAEOLOGY, GUATEMALA CITY).

In our overview, time and again we have come across Yaxchilán and Piedras Negras, the cities that vied with each other for control over the Usumacinta region.

The dynasty of Yaxchilán, the splendid city set in a meander of the Usumacinta, was founded by Yoaat B'alam ("Penis Jaguar") in AD 359.

The city continued to develop, probably controlled by Tikal, and made a name for itself through its significant military activity in the 5th and 6th centuries (though with mixed results), mainly against Piedras Negras and Bonampak, but also against Tikal, Calakmul and cities in the Selva Lacandona area. Nevertheless, it is thought that throughout much of the Classic Period Yaxchilán was controlled by the nearby city of Piedras Negras.

Located just 25 miles away, Piedras Negras began to develop toward the end of the 3rd century, and for at least 200 years it was a little kingdom constantly in conflict with Yaxchilán. It may also have been subject to the supreme authority of the king of Calakmul for a certain period of time. At the beginning of the 7th century Piedras Negras began to compete with Palenque to gain control over the

lower course of the Usumacinta and probably ended up dominating the nearby kingdoms of Yaxchilán, Bonampak and Lacanhá.

It is possible that Piedras Negras' rise to power was also aided by its alliance with Calakmul when Yuknoom the Great ruled the capital of Kaan.

During the reign of K'inich Yo'nal Ahk II ("Sun God? Turtle", AD 687–729), Piedras Negras' control over the Usumacinta region began to wane, probably due to the simultaneous crisis of Calakmul, defeated by Tikal, and the growing power of Palenque and Yaxchilán, ruled by Itzamnaaj B'alam II.

Itzamnaaj B'alam II, who ruled Yaxchilán from 681 to 742, was responsible for the city's renaissance, marked by a long string of military victories against the region's minor sites, expanding Yaxchilán's territory to the borders of its eternal rival Piedras Negras. It is not surprising, in fact, that the inscriptions commissioned by Itzamnaaj B'alam II "forget" to mention the city's defeat in 726 at the hands of Piedras Negras, when one of the vassals of the Yaxchilán king was taken prisoner.

Temple 23 was built during the reign of Itzamnaaj B'alam II. The carved lintels from this temple, dedicated to one of his wives, can unquestionably be counted among the most exquisite works in the history of Maya art. The three lintels depict three rituals involving the woman, who is portrayed with her husband: in the first one she is having a vision, in the second one she is pulling a thorn-studded cord through her tongue during a bloodletting ritual, and in the third she is giving her husband a jaguar helmet.

Itzamnaaj B'alam II died in 742 at the age of 90, unleashing a dynastic struggle that left the Yaxchilán throne vacant for an

entire decade. During this period the city probably fell under the control of Piedras Negras, given the fact that in 749 one of its nobles (probably a governor during the interregnum) attended the celebration of the twenty-year reign of Ruler 4 of Piedras Negras, under whom the city consolidated its power in the region.

The Yaxchilán interregnum came to an end with the ascent of Bird Jaguar IV to the throne. This king worked tireless to affirm his legitimacy and reinforce it through military campaigns against minor sites that were probably more valuable as propaganda than in real terms. In 759, however, the capture of a nobleman with a title typical of Piedras Negras reveals increasingly important conflict, probably to free itself of the oppression of its powerful neighbor. In effect, the flurry of architectural activity during his reign seems to indicate that Yaxchilán had gained its independence and amassed substantial wealth. It fell to his son Itzamnaaj B'alam III to defend the status the city had achieved. He did this through numerous military undertakings, in an era in which Yaxchilán came to rule directly over important cities like Lacanhá and Bonampak. At the same time, Piedras Negras was consolidating its control over the

region through wars against Pomoná and other minor sites.

The victories of the two cities probably rekindled their old rivalry and led to their final confrontation: in 808 K'inich Tatb'u Skull III of Yaxchilán defeated and killed Ruler 7 of Piedras Negras, which was destroyed and abandoned a few years later. But Yaxchilán's victory was a hollow one: the monument recounting this battle was the last to be erected in the city, which was abandoned forever just a few years later.

- THE DECAPITATED STATUE OF BIRD JAGUAR, THE CITY'S MOST FAMOUS KING, IS LOCATED IN BUILDING 33 AT YAXCHILÁN, IN A NARROW ENTRANCE ARCADE WITH A "FALSE VAULT."

124 - YAXCHILÁN, IN CHIAPAS, WAS THE CAPITAL OF ONE OF THE MOST POWERFUL KINGDOMS IN THE USUMACINTA REGION. ITS MONUMENTAL CENTER IS SITUATED IN A SPLENDID MEANDER OF THIS RIVER, WHICH MARKS THE MODERN-DAY BORDER BETWEEN MEXICO AND GUATEMALA.

124-125 - THE KING KNOWN AS BIRD JAGUAR, DRESSED FOR WAR, IS PORTRAYED WITH HIS WIFE ON LINTEL 41 FROM YAXCHILÁN. THE INSCRIPTION IN THE CORNER CONTAINS CALENDRICAL INFORMATION (BRITISH MUSEUM, LONDON).

126 - The image of a monkey can be noted on Lintel 48 from Yaxchilán. Most of the bas-reliefs from this city decorated the lintels of monumental buildings.

127 - Lintel 16 from Yaxchilán portrays the king known as Bird Jaguar dressed as a warrior, alongside his prisoner of war Chac Cib Tok, captured on February 10, 752 (British Museum, London).

128

128 - LINTEL 26 FROM YAXCHILÁN PORTRAYS KING ITZAMNAAJ B'ALAM II WITH HIS WIFE, WHO IS HANDING HIM A WAR HELMET SHAPED LIKE THE HEAD OF A JAGUAR (NATIONAL MUSEUM OF ANTHROPOLOGY, MEXICO CITY).

129 - THE QUEEN'S FACE IS DECORATED WITH FINE SCARS NEAR THE CORNERS OF HER MOUTH. LADY XOOK WAS THE WIFE OF ITZAMNAAJ B'ALAM II (NATIONAL MUSEUM OF ANTHROPOLOGY, MEXICO CITY).

AUTOSACRIFICE

Autosacrifice, one of the most widespread ritual practices among the Maya elite, consisted of various forms of bloodletting that were supposed to lead to a state of ecstasy. The most common forms of bloodletting involved perforating body parts (genitals, tongue, calves, ears, etc.) using stingray spines or replicas made of jadeite or obsidian; even the instruments themselves were worshiped as deities in the form of the Perforator God. Maya inscriptions tell us that rulers practiced autosacrificial rituals during the most important ceremonial celebrations, such as coronations, births and the presentation of heirs to the throne.

Two of the lintels from Temple 23 at Yaxchilán are decorated with some of the finest images of autosacrifice found in the Maya area. In one, the queen of the city is shown running a thorn-studded rope through her tongue, and the blood dripping down the cord is collected in a bowl filled with strips of fig-bark paper. The other lintel shows the effects of the ceremony (although it actually refers to another ritual occasion). The blood-soaked paper has been set afire and the column of smoke rising from it is transformed into the body of the Vision Serpent. The image of the ancestor evoked by the rite of the queen – who is depicted in the midst of her vision, her head thrown back – emerges from the serpent's mouth.

Autosacrifice, which the rulers performed chiefly through ritual penis perforation, was thus a way to demonstrate the shamanic abilities of the kings, who could communicate with their dead ancestors and thus legitimize their right to rule. The importance of these rituals as part of the Maya ideology of royalty is also indicated by the large number of bloodletting instruments that were placed in royal tombs.

The practice of bloodletting was common throughout Mesoamerica and endured until the early colonial period. In his *Relación de las Cosas de Yucatán* (1566), the Franciscan Diego de Landa, Bishop of Yucatán, wrote: "They would gather in a temple… and, lined in up a row, they would pierce oblique holes on the sides of their virile members, and passing the largest possible amount of cord through them they remained there, strung together, and they would sprinkle the blood of all those parts on the demon…."

130 - THIS CLOSE-UP OF THE DECORATION OF A CYLINDRICAL MAYA VASE SHOWS THE MAIZE GOD SEATED IN A TYPICAL POSITION WITH HIS LEGS CROSSED, AS HE OFFERS BLOOD OBTAINED FROM THE RITUAL OF AUTOSACRIFICE (FOUNDATION FOR THE ADVANCEMENT OF MESOAMERICAN STUDIES, FLORIDA).

131 - LINTEL 24 FROM YAXCHILÁN ILLUSTRATES THE RITUAL OF AUTOSACRIFICE. LADY K'ABAL XOOK IS PULLING A THORN-STUDDED CORD THROUGH HER TONGUE, COLLECTING THE BLOOD IN A BOWL SET AT HER HUSBAND'S FEET (BRITISH MUSEUM, LONDON).

132-133 - THE SCENE PAINTED ON THIS CYLINDRICAL VASE FROM THE CLASSIC PERIOD PORTRAYS A KING PIERCING HIS PENIS WITH A LARGE PERFORATOR (RIGHT), WHILE A PRIEST OFFERS BLOOD-SOAKED PAPER BEFORE A MASK OF K'AWIIL, THE GOD OF ROYAL BLOOD (PRIVATE COLLECTION).

134 TOP - THIS SCULPTURE DECORATES ONE OF COPÁN'S MONUMENTAL BUILDINGS. AT COPÁN, SCULPTURE IN THE ROUND ACHIEVED EXTRAORDINARY LEVELS OF ARTISTRY AND CAME TO REPRESENT ONE OF THE MOST DISTINCTIVE MAYA STYLES.

134 BOTTOM LEFT - THIS ALTAR AT COPÁN IS SET AT THE FOOT OF STELA D AND IS SCULPTED IN THE FORM OF A SKULL TO REPRESENT THE DEAD SUN OF THE UNDERWORLD. OFFERINGS DEDICATED TO THE KING WERE PLACED ON THE ALTARS.

134 BOTTOM RIGHT - FREESTANDING STELAE DEPICTING THE VARIOUS KINGS THAT RULED THE CITY RISE IN THE MONUMENTAL PLAZA OF COPÁN. MOST OF THEM PORTRAY WAXAKLAJUUN UB'AAH K'AWIIL, THE MOST RENOWNED KING OF COPÁN.

134-135 - ALTAR G1 AT COPÁN DEPICTS THE TWO-HEADED DRAGON, AN ANIMAL MANIFESTATION OF THE SUPREME HEAVENLY DEITY. THE SPHERE JUTTING FROM THE CENTRAL INSCRIPTION IS A PORTRAYAL OF THE SUN FOLLOWING ITS PATH ON THE DRAGON'S FEATHERED BODY.

135 BOTTOM - IN AD 756 THE RULER K'AK' YIPYAJ CHAN K'AWIIL HAD HIMSELF PORTRAYED ON STELA M AT THE FOOT OF THE MAJESTIC HIEROGLYPHIC STAIRCASE OF TEMPLE 26, WHICH HE HAD COMPLETED THE YEAR BEFORE. THE STAIRCASE, WHICH HAS THE LONGEST KNOWN MAYA INSCRIPTION, RECOUNTS THE HISTORY OF THE CITY DYNASTY.

The city of Copán (Honduras) may well be the most impressive of the ancient Maya cities, not only because of its magnificent acropolis, but also for the beauty and elegance of its numerous city monuments. Quiriguá, boasting colossal 25-foot-tall stelae that are unique in Maya art, is only about 50 miles away. Given their proximity, it is not surprising that the histories of these two cities in the southernmost part of the Maya area — a region rich in natural resources — were entwined.

Despite the fact that the region of Copán was densely populated even in the Preclassic Period, we know that its dynastic foundation has been traced to AD 426, when K'inich Yax K'uk' Mo' ("Great Sun First Quetzal Macaw") rose to the throne in a way that seems to connect him to Tikal and Teotihuacán. Thus, this links him with the wave of dynasties established with Teotihuacán's "entry" into the territory of Tikal and with the reign of Siyaj Chan K'awiil. The first king of nearby Quiriguá, known as Tok Casper, was also crowned during this ceremony, held was at a site that has yet to be identified.

The excavation of a series of tunnels inside the Copán Acropolis has allowed archaeologists to discover a complete architectural sequence whose initial phases date back to the reign of Yax K'uk Mo'. Unsurprisingly, the architectural features of the structures he built are typical of Teotihuacán and Tikal, in keeping with his supposed "outside" origin, which analysis of the bones found in his rich tomb also seems to confirm. Teotihuacán-style elements were also found in the later tomb of one of his wives, a local woman who was buried with remarkable furnishings inside a Maya-style structure that effectively must have been a shrine commemorating the dead king, whose name appears in a large polychrome bas-relief.

The numerous successors of Yax K'uk Mo' ruled over an opulent city. Thanks to the rich local environment — and possibly also to the fact that it was far from the turbulent and politically unstable Petén area — Copán developed uneventfully for centuries, without any dynastic crises or military conflicts. It also established important diplomatic and trade relations with the cities of the Motagua Basin and the southern part of Belize. Nearby Quiriguá must have played an important role in this trade network. Because it was located in the Motagua Basin, it probably served as the link between Copán, to which it was subordinate politically, and the Caribbean area of Belize.

Quiriguá also managed to recover from a natural disaster, after a flood destroyed its monumental center in the late 6th or early 7th century. It was immediately rebuilt nearby, on the banks of the Motagua River, and port facilities were also constructed.

During these centuries of well-being, the monumental center of Copán was gradually adorned with splendid buildings, the most important of which is the magnificent Rosalia.

Built in the second half of the 7th century over the tomb of Yax K'uk' Mo', this structure is decorated with polychrome bas-relief stuccowork.

The stelae with the portraits of kings gradually developed into the typical Copán style in which the entire figure of the ruler is sculpted almost in the round and is literally "inundated" with detailing and attributes, in a style that looks overly ornate and "baroque" by modern standards.

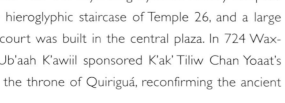

Waxaklajuun Ub'aah K'awiil ("Eighteen Images of K'awiil") was unquestionably the most important and celebrated king in the history of Copán, and he ascended to the throne in 695, the same year that Tikal was finally getting its revenge against Calakmul. During the long rein of Waxaklajuun Ub'aah K'awiil Copán reached the height of its splendor, and the monumental center was adorned with an extensive series of stelae portraying the ruler donning the symbols of various deities and engaged in various ritual practices.

The ruler had the city's long dynastic history sculpted along the hieroglyphic staircase of Temple 26, and a large new ball court was built in the central plaza. In 724 Waxaklajuun Ub'aah K'awiil sponsored K'ak' Tiliw Chan Yoaat's ascent to the throne of Quiriguá, reconfirming the ancient supremacy that the kings of Copán exercised over the "vassal" rulers of the nearby city.

When Waxaklajuun Ub'aah K'awiil was at the height of his power after ruling for 43 years, the unthinkable happened: in 738 he was defeated in battle by none other than K'ak Tiliw Chan Yoaat, and six days later he was beheaded on the altars of Quiriguá.

The details of this sensational rebellion are unclear, but there are signs that it may have been "sponsored" by Calakmul, possibly to recover from its recent defeat by attempting to topple the political organization of Tikal and its allies, near and far.

This unexpected defeat plunged Copán into a deep crisis. Its political power fell apart and the city witnessed the ascent of Quiriguá, which gained control over the rich region of Motagua following this victory.

In effect, K'ak Tiliw Chan Yoaat was quick to display the signs of his capital's new status.

The monumental center was renovated, imitating Copán's architecture in many respects, as part of a sweeping architectural and propagandist program designed to link Quiriguá's renaissance with the creation of the universe.

In the largest plaza in the Maya world, the ruler erected a series of enormous stelae/portraits – one every five years – in direct competition with the ones that Waxaklajuun Ub'aah K'awiil had erected in the plaza at Copán.

Copán's distinctive zoomorphic altars were also "copied" in a colossal form by K'ak Tiliw Chan Yoaat and, after his death in 785, by his successor Sky Xul, yielding some of the most beautiful and impressive sculptures in the history of Maya art.

136 - THIS CLOSE-UP SHOWS A BAS-RELIEF FROM A BENCH IN TEMPLE 11, AT COPÁN, WHICH YAX PASAJ CHAN YOAAT HAD SCULPTED IN AD 775.

136-137 - ON STELA B, WAXAKLAJUUN UB'AAH K'AWIIL – MASKED WITH A FAKE SHELL BEARD – IS PORTRAYED CLOSE TO A MYTHICAL PLACE KNOWN AS "MACAW MOUNTAIN."

Despite the triumphs of its intrusive and ambitious neighbor, Copán apparently managed to recover, and new monuments were built during the reign of Waxaklajuun Ub'aah K'awiil's two successors. One of the most important was the extension of the hieroglyphic staircase (making it the longest inscription in the Maya world), decorated with statues portraying five Copán rulers dressed as Teotihuacán warriors to evoke the city's ancient splendor. During the reign of Yax Pasaj Chan Yoaat ("First Dawned Sky Lightning God"), the 16th successor of Yax K'uk' Mo' and the son of a princess from Palenque, a new altar was set before the temple, which had gradually been enlarged over the tomb of the dynasty's founder. This was the famous Altar Q, with the portraits of all 16 kings of Copán along the sides. For all their splendor, however, these monuments could do little to ward off a severe

economic crisis, which was probably triggered by overpopulation of the valley and land erosion; the crisis seems to have affected both Copán and Quiriguá. Evidence of a "rapprochement" between the two cities seems to suggest an attempt to join forces to deal with a situation that was becoming increasingly unbearable. But to no avail: the last dated monument at Quiriguá indicates the year AD 810, whereas the altar dedicated in February of 822 during the coronation of the last king of Copán, Ukit Took' ("Patron? of Flint") was never finished, testifying to Copán's demise.

140-141 - DETAIL OF THE DECORATION OF THE HOUSE OF THE SCRIBES AT COPÁN, WITH A SCULPTURE DEPICTING ONE OF THE SCRIBES' SUPERNATURAL PATRONS IN THE FORM OF A MONKEY.

141 - THANKS ALSO TO THE AVAILABILITY OF HIGH-QUALITY LIMESTONE, COPÁN'S SCULPTORS PRODUCED EXQUISITE AND VERY EXPRESSIVE WORKS, LIKE THE TWO FACES PORTRAYED HERE. THEY WERE PART OF THE DECORATIONS OF A MONUMENTAL BUILDING.

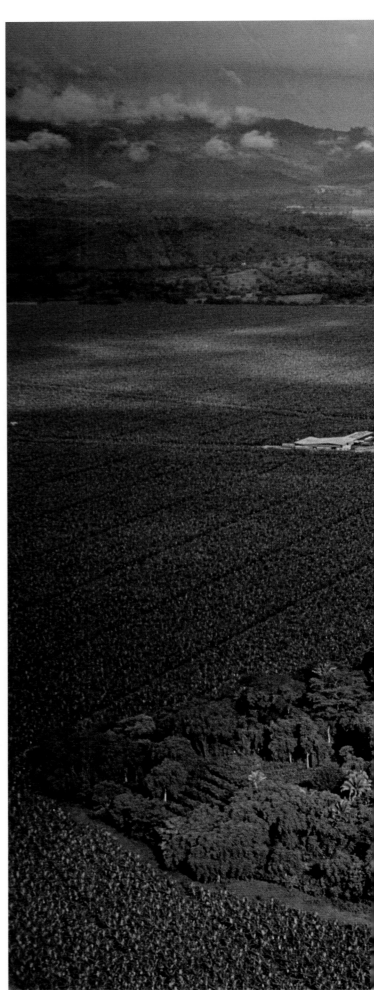

142 - THE SCULPTURES TYPICAL OF QUIRIGUÁ INCLUDE ZOOMORPHIC ALTARS, LARGE BLOCKS OF LIMESTONE SCULPTED IN THE ROUND (SUCH AS ZOOMORPH P, ABOVE), AND THE COLOSSAL STELAE IN THE MAIN PLAZA, WHICH ARE THE TALLEST ONES IN THE MAYA AREA (BELOW, A CLOSE-UP OF STELA D).

142-143 - THIS AERIAL VIEW SHOWS THE MONUMENTAL CENTER OF QUIRIGUÁ, IN THE MOTAGUA VALLEY (GUATEMALA). LONG RULED BY NEARBY COPÁN, QUIRIGUÁ FINALLY GAINED ITS FREEDOM WITH THE CELEBRATED MILITARY VICTORY OF AD 738, LED BY THE RULER K'AK TILIW CHAN YOAAT.

THE BALLGAME

Playing ball was one of the most important and widespread ritual games in Mesoamerica, and its practice had important political implications. As we have already seen, the first Mesoamerican ball court was built at Paso de la Amada, on the Chiapas coast, in 1600 BC, during a key period in the rise of hierarchical societies. In the Maya world as well, playing ball was closely related to royalty. Monumental bas-reliefs often depict rulers playing ball and, in some cases, they are dressed like their heroic prototypes, the twins Ju'n'Ajaw and Yax B'alam, who went to play ball against the gods of the underworld. It is likely that the ball court, conceptually designed as the gateway to the underworld, also became the stage for "fake" matches that were actually forms of sacrifice, in which prisoners of war lost the game and were then sacrificed. Several sculptures also show the appalling method used to perform one of these sacrifices: the prisoner, his hands and feet bound behind his back, was thrown from the side staircases of the court as if he were a ball.

Ball playing must have been particularly widespread in the Mixe-Zoque area of the Gulf. Some of the Classic settlements here had over 20 ball courts, and stone reproductions of the accessories used for the game (referred to as "yokes," "axes," and "palms") were created with extraordinary ability, making them veritable masterpieces.

144 - THIS SPLENDID TERRACOTTA FIGURINE FROM THE NORTHERN PETÉN AREA OF GUATEMALA PORTRAYS A BALLPLAYER (PRIVATE COLLECTION).

144-145 - CLASSIC MAYA VASES OFTEN DEPICTED BALLGAMES WITH JUST TWO PLAYERS, WHO WERE EITHER RULERS OR DEITIES. THE FIGURES WEAR DAZZLING GARMENTS AND LAVISH HEADDRESSES, AND THEY ARE OFTEN SHOWN WITH LARGE STAIRCASES IN THE BACKGROUND (CHRYSLER MUSEUM OF ARTS, NORFOLK, VIRGINIA).

We do not have an accurate idea of the rules of the game, due also to the fact that the few Europeans who had a chance to observe matches during the period of the Spanish conquest focused almost entirely on the rubber ball itself. Rubber, which did not exist in Europe at the time, astonished observers – accustomed to leather or rag balls – because of the fact that it could bounce. We know, however, that players had to hit the heavy rubber ball with their shoulders or sides, which were protected by wide belts, and that the ball could not hit the ground before reached the other half of the court. Classic ball courts, which had slanted walls to allow the ball to rebound, were fitted with round

"markers" set on the playing field, which must have been used for scoring points.

The teams in the Classic Period must have been quite small and images of the games often show just two players. Instead, the courts in the Postclassic period, which were fitted with round rings mounted on vertical walls like basketball hoops, were much larger and could accommodate bigger teams.

Ballplayers had to be excellent leapers: virtually acrobats. The Europeans were so impressed that a team of Aztec players was brought to Madrid to demonstrate the men's prowess before Charles V.

146 - The carving on this "axe" from Veracruz shows a predator pecking at a human skull. The "axes" were ritual instruments associated with the ballgame (National Museum of Archaeology, Guatemala City).

147 - This marker is from the ball court at La Esperanza, near the site of Chinkultic, in Chiapas. It portrays a ballplayer surrounded by an inscription dated AD 591 (National Museum of Anthropology, Mexico City).

148-149 - In many Classic
depictions, the ball is much larger
than the ones known
archaeologically or described by
chroniclers from later periods.
This may be represent aesthetic
exaggeration, but some authors
have also suggested that inflatable
rubber balls were used (Toniná
Site Museum).

149 bottom - The stone "yokes"
represent the ballplayers'
protective belts, which were
probably made of leather. The
picture shows a yoke sculpted in
the shape of a frog. This item is
from central Veracruz
(Indianapolis Museum of Art).

150 AND 151 - THESE TERRACOTTA
FIGURINES PORTRAY TWO BALLPLAYERS
IN THE TYPICAL POSITION WITH ONE KNEE
ON THE GROUND. THE PLAYERS WORE
ENORMOUS BELTS TO PROTECT THEIR
SIDES FROM IMPACT WITH THE SOLID
RUBBER BALL, WHICH PROBABLY
WEIGHED SEVERAL POUNDS (NATIONAL
MUSEUM OF ANTHROPOLOGY, MEXICO
CITY).

152 AND 153 – THESE FIGURINES FROM JAINA REPRESENT HIGH-RANKING PEOPLE DRESSED AS BALLPLAYERS. BECAUSE OF THE ASSOCIATION BETWEEN THE BALLGAME AND THE FOUNDATION MYTH OF MAYA ROYALTY, RULERS OFTEN PLAYED RITUAL GAMES IN WHICH THEY REENACTED THE STORY OF THE TWINS OF THE *POPOL VUH*, THE PROTOTYPES OF MAYA ROYALTY (NATIONAL MUSEUM OF ANTHROPOLOGY, MEXICO CITY).

154-155 - The Building of the Five Floors is the most famous structure at Edzná, in Campeche, and its architectural style demonstrates that at the turn of the 1st millennium this important Yucatec city became part of the Puuc Maya world.

154 bottom - The North Temple of the Great Acropolis at Edzná rises alongside the Building of the Five Floors and dates back to between AD 850 and 1100.

155 - The tapered shape of the Classic pyramids at Cobá (Quintana Roo) is unique among the Maya sites of the Yucatán Peninsula. This suggests that the powerful city had important relations with coeval Maya cities in the southern lowlands, such as Tikal, where this architectural style was very common.

Though the historical events examined so far have been concentrated mainly in the Petén region, this does not mean that the Yucatán Peninsula played a minor role in the development of the Classic Maya civilization. After the important advances of the Preclassic Period, which we have already examined, the Yucatán Peninsula developed uninterruptedly. During the Classic Period the central and northern part of the peninsula was essentially divided into two main cultural regions: the eastern one, closely tied to Petén, where Cobá was a leading city on a par with other important centers such as Kohunlich and Dzibanché; the northwestern one, which was distinguished by the great development of sites like Edzná, Ek Balam and Dzibichaltún.

The site of Cobá (Quintana Roo), composed of separate architectural groups dotting the low-lying Yucatán rainforest near large lagoons, is distinguished by the fact that its monuments most closely resemble the style of the ones found in the Petén area. Its tall pyramids, as well as the numerous stelae with bas-relief images of kings and queens trampling on prisoners of war, testify to the importance of the contacts that this Yucatec capital maintained with the powers of the Petén lowlands to the south.

Edzná (Campeche) was indubitably one of the most important Yucatec Maya settlements and it was occupied uninterruptedly from the Middle Preclassic (600 BC) to the Postclassic Period (AD 1450). During the Early Classic period, the city maintained important trade relations with the southern lowland areas, which are reflected in various architectural elements and above all in the exquisite stucco masks, depicting the Sun King, that decorate Structure 414. After AD 700 Edzná became an important Puuc Maya site. It was during this period that the famous "Building of the Five Floors" – now the city's most famous architectural structure – was constructed.

THE CLASSIC MAYA OF THE YUCATÁN PENINSULA

156-157 - This view shows the South Plaza of Ek Balam in Yucatán. The monumental building known as "The Twins" can be seen in the middle of the picture. To the right, the city's ball court is visible in the foreground.

157 top - The photograph shows the altar of the stelae of Dzibichaltún, in Yucatán, one of the most long-lived Maya cities: it prospered from the Middle Preclassic Period until just a few decades before the Spanish conquest. The Temple of the Seven Dolls is visible in the background.

157 bottom - This monumental building at Ek Balam is referred to as the Oval Palace. The Yucatec city enjoyed a long period of prosperity between AD 700 and 1000, forging relations with Cobá and then with Puuc cities such as Chichén Itzá.

The site of Ek Balam, which flourished between 700 and AD 1000, also deserves mention, particularly because of the extraordinary stucco frieze decorating the city's large acropolis and depicting the ruler Ukit Kan Le'k Tok' emerging from the mouth of a monstrous creature.

Dzibichaltún, which was also occupied since the Pre-classic Period, reached its apogee after AD 700, and all the dated monuments found at this site are from the 9th century. Famous city monuments such as the Temple of the Seven Dolls were built during this period.

One of the most distinctive features of the Yucatec sites – although it is not exclusive to this area – is the presence of countless *sacbeob*, the "white roads" or causeways that linked the different settlements. They were probably built to seal alliances between these areas, and to promote the trade contacts and diplomatic-ceremonial activities that these alliances implied.

RÍO BEC AND CHENES: TWO YUCATEC STYLES

In the southernmost part of the Yucatán Peninsula, the Classic Period saw the development of two unique architectural styles that, in a certain way, represented the "link" between the Petén area and the northern part of the peninsula. In the latter area, toward the end of the Classic Period the Puuc region came to the fore as the most dynamic and politically stable region of the Maya world.

The Río Bec style developed in the southern areas of the states of Campeche and Quintana Roo during the Late Classic Period (AD 600–900) and it is well represented at sites such as Río Bec (after which this style is named), Xpuhil, Hormiguero and Chicanná. Recent studies of several settlements such as Nadzcaan have demonstrated that the Río Bec style developed

progressively at sites that had previously shared the Petén style and probably represented the northernmost boundary of Calakmul's sphere of influence. The most distinctive element of the Río Bec style is the use of pyramids with "false" towers and a front staircase serving a purely decorative purpose. The tall crest decorating the top of these structures is clearly a feature copied from the crests typical of Petén architecture. Another element commonly found in Río Bec buildings can be seen in the temple façades, decorated with intricate limestone mosaics that give them the shape of the gaping maw of the Earth Monster, magnificently exemplified by Temple 2 at Hochob.

The Chenes architectural style developed a little further north, in close contact with the Río Bec area. This style can be seen at sites such as Hochob, Dzibilnocac and Tabasqueño. Façades with zoomorphic openings were common in this area as well, and they often had statues jutting from them. This feature would later become typical of the nearby Puuc region, the hub of peninsular cultural developments toward the end of the Classic Period.

158 - "THE TOWER," WHICH HOLDS THE
ROYAL TOMB OF UKIT KAN LE'K, HAS A
ZOOMORPHIC FAÇADE WITH A STUCCO BAS-
RELIEF THAT CHARACTERIZES IT AS THE
GAPING MAW OF THE MOUNTAIN OR WITZ
MONSTER.

158-159 - THE STUCCO FAÇADE OF
THE TOMB OF UKIT KAN LE'K
PRESENTS SEVERAL FIGURES IN THE
ROUND, SUCH AS THIS ONE OF A MAN
SEATED IN THE EYE OF THE WITZ
MONSTER.

THE PUUC CITIES

Between AD 700 and 1000, the region of the low hills of Puuc in the northwestern part of the Yucatán Peninsula enjoyed a period of extraordinary cultural efflorescence. Dynamic political entities arose here, governed by cities such as Uxmal, Kabah, Sayil and Chichén Itzá, whose monumental centers were distinguished by a new architectural style. The most distinctive trait of this style involved the use of buildings whose façades were decorated with elaborate mosaics made of limestone blocks forming intricate decorative motifs, with fretwork, lattices, series of columns and enormous masks of the gods.

It is not clear yet if the Puuc development was related to the migration of groups – the Chontal or Putún Maya – from the Gulf Coast. According to several sources, lineages like the Itzá and Xiw came to the Yucatán Peninsula between the 7th and 8th centuries, but other sources date this event to the centuries shortly thereafter.

In any event, it is clear that during the early centuries of Puuc development Uxmal was the leading center of the northern part of the peninsula, probably through a close alliance with the cities of Kabah and Nojpat. Many of the monuments we can see today in this large capital date back to the reign of Lord Chaak, who ruled Uxmal from the late 9th to early 10th century.

He erected the famous Nunnery Quadrangle, an architectural complex composed of four buildings whose façades are decorated with motifs alluding to creation myths and their connection with the ideology of sacred royalty. It is likely, however, that the royal residence or "house of the government council" was the House of the Governor, whose façade is oriented to face the point where Venus rises over the southern end. A throne shaped like a two-headed jaguar is set in front of the temple, and we can easily imagine that the ruler would sit there during this celestial event, reinforcing the ancient association between the royal figure and the war star. The impressive Pyramid of the Magician, whose rounded corners make it unique in Maya architecture, was built a short time later.

160 top - The monumental city of Uxmal, in Yucatán, is dominated by the sheer size of the Pyramid of the Magician. Uxmal, which flourished between the 8th and the 10th centuries, was one of the most important Puuc Maya cities.

160 bottom - The Nunnery Quadrangle is one of the main architectural complexes at Uxmal. It is composed of four large buildings set around a quadrangular patio, and was erected between AD 900 and 910 by Lord Chaak, the city's most important ruler.

161 - This mask decorates the corner of a building in the Nunnery Quadrangle. The long snake-like nose is distinctive of Chac, the Rain God.

162-163 - The Pyramid of the
Magician, which is over 130 feet (40
m) tall, is the most impressive
building in Uxmal. Its east side, with
a small decorated temple, dominates
the complex known as the
Quadrangle of the Birds.

163 top - The Nunnery
Quadrangle is composed of
buildings whose decorations
allude to the creation myth: this
mythological cycle may have been
associated with the city's political
order.

163 CENTER LEFT - THE EAST BUILDING OF THE NUNNERY QUADRANGLE IS A LOW, ELONGATED STRUCTURE TYPICAL OF THE ARCHITECTURE OF THE END OF THE CLASSIC PERIOD IN THE YUCATÁN AREA AS WELL AS OTHER PARTS OF THE MAYA AND MESOAMERICAN REGIONS.

163 CENTER RIGHT - IN THIS DECORATION OF A BUILDING AT UXMAL, THE FIGURE OF THE FEATHERED SERPENT STANDS OUT, DEMONSTRATING THE GROWING "MEXICAN" INFLUENCE THAT REACHED THE YUCATÁN TOWARD THE END OF THE CLASSIC PERIOD.

163 BOTTOM - THE HOUSE OF THE GOVERNOR WAS PROBABLY THE POPOL NA, OR SEAT OF CITY GOVERNMENT. IN FRONT OF THE FAÇADE, THERE IS A THRONE IN THE SHAPE OF A TWO-HEADED JAGUAR: THE RULER WOULD SIT HERE DURING THE TRANSIT OF VENUS TO ITS SOUTHERNMOST POINT.

Other elements typical of Puuc architecture include multistoried buildings like the ones at Sayil and Kabah, and arches set at the beginning of the *sacbeob*. Notable examples of these arches can be seen at Kabah and Labná; the latter is a gem of Maya architecture.

Political relations extended outside the actual Puuc area, as demonstrated by the diffusion of Puuc elements in the architecture of Edzná – notably the Building of the Five Floors – and Chichén Itzá, where buildings such as the Nunnery, the Annex, the Church, the Red House and Akab Dzib are some of the best-known examples of Puuc architecture.

It is likely that Uxmal's control over the Puuc area was backed by an alliance with Chichén Itzá, the city that, short-

ly thereafter, took advantage of the political upheaval that shook the Puuc Maya area and developed into the most important center of power of the Maya world.

Puuc sites flourished until the end of the 10th century, when new cultural elements reached the Yucatán Peninsula, revolutionizing the area's political organization and ushering in the era we refer to as the Postclassic Period.

164-165 - MASKS OF THE GODS AND GROUPS OF COLUMNS ALTERNATE ON THE FAÇADE OF THE THREE-STORY STRUCTURE OF THE GREAT PALACE IN SAYIL, ON THE YUCATÁN PENINSULA.

165 top - THE LABNÁ ARCH IS ONE OF THE MOST FAMOUS PUUC MONUMENTS.

THE DEMISE OF THE CLASSIC MAYA: COLLAPSE OR TRANSFORMATION?

The "collapse" of the Classic Maya civilization is a topic that has been debated endlessly, but a truly convincing explanation has yet to emerge. Before we can examine this event we must clear up a number of recurrent misunderstandings. First of all, as opposed to what is commonly thought this "collapse" was not a sweeping occurrence that wiped out an entire civilization. In fact, it was limited to a specific area (the southern lowlands) that, though of primary importance, was merely one of the large regions in which the Classic Maya civilization developed. Indeed, as the southern lowlands were declining, other regions were enjoying their golden age, "collapsing" over a century later or – in some cases – not at all. Notable examples of this include the Puuc sites in northern Yucatán, the ones along the southeastern coast

of the peninsula like Dzibanché, Kohunlich, Lamanai, Altun Há and Nohmul, and the ones in the region of Río de la Pasión, such as Seibal and Altar de Sacrificios. Secondly, the collapse that struck the southern lowlands between AD 800 and 900 was not something new that had never happened before. As we have already seen, at the end of the Late Preclassic Period an enormous crisis led to the disappearance of the large states of northern Petén, such as the one at El Mirador.

Another element that is often underestimated involves the repercussions that the political events in other Mesoamerican regions may have had on the central Maya area. Teotihuacán was torched in AD 650 and no longer predominated in central Mexico. Subsequently, a chain of "collapses" struck other important Classic sites such as Cholula and Monte Albán, the important capital of the Zapotec state of Oaxaca, sparking migration and profoundly redressing the political balance: this would inevitably have affected the Maya area.

Nevertheless, it is undeniable that the collapse of the southern lowlands was a phenomenon of enormous significance, putting an end to a system that had dominated the area for a millennium and triggering a decline in population from which the southern lowlands would never recover. The causes that are generally cited to explain this collapse essentially fall into two categories: internal sociopolitical factors and external environmental ones. Among the former, we can cite the old theory of a peasant revolt against an increasingly demanding noble class. Likewise, there is the more recent observation that, starting in the 7th century, central power seems to have weakened progressively, as reflected by an increase in the elite classes. This is demonstrated by the fact that monuments

166 - On the east façade of the Codz Pop in Kabah, there was a series of sculptures depicting the city rulers. This face clearly shows how Puuc Maya art moved away from the elements of Classic Maya Art (National Museum of Anthropology, Mexico

167 - These two statues are still in place on the west façade of the Codz Pop. The statues, which are larger than life-size, are composed of assembled stone blocks. The background is composed of quetzal feathers.

frequently mention individuals who, though they were not kings, boasted the title of ajaw and were portrayed on monuments that, centuries before, would have borne only the effigies of supreme rulers.

The theories of external ecological-environmental causes have recently gained new impetus. According to these theories, population growth and more intensive farming — which, in turn, would have impoverished the soil and caused erosion — were the main factors in this crisis, exacerbated by dry spells that seem to have been concentrated toward the end of the Classic Period.

Each of these hypotheses is confirmed at some sites but not others, and as a result it is difficult to consider any of them as the single basic cause of the collapse of the Maya civilization. Though the solution to this problem is still far off, it must undoubtedly be sought in the convergence of various factors. The political system of the Classic Maya — involving a continuous cycle of alliances and rifts, collapses and rebirths — struggled to deal with a particularly critical moment that may also have been triggered by environmental factors. To respond to the crisis, these populations gave the individual noble lines greater independence, and enhanced political and economic competition. The latter was reflected in increased warring and changes in warfare methods, which became increasingly destructive toward the end of the Classic Period, as demonstrated at the site of Cancuén. In the meantime, the "non-Classic" Maya groups like the Chontal of the lower coast of the Gulf of Mexico began to penetrate the lowlands. They introduced cultural elements typical of central Mexico, as well as new forms of government that were better suited to the multiethnic character of the social structures that were formed following the migrations characterizing the end of the Late Classic Period.

In this kind of scenario, the ancient sovereign power of the ajaw would have revealed its complete inability to cope with enormously changed social and economic conditions. The power that had lasted over 1000 years rapidly disintegrated, triggering an endless downward spiral that culminated with the abandonment of monumental centers by a population that migrated toward rural areas, possibly also quite far away. In these distant areas, which had been "marginal" with respect to the great powers of Petén, these groups ultimately adapted to new conditions and rose to new heights in the centuries that followed.

168 TOP - THE MAIN PALACE IN KABAH, WHICH IS SIMILAR TO OTHER BUILDINGS IN THE PUUC CITY, OVERLOOKS THE SAME PLAZA AS THE CODZ POP. A STELA RISES IN THE MIDDLE OF THE PLAZA.

168 bottom and 168-169 - The masks of the Codz Pop were traditionally interpreted as portrayals of Chac, the Rain God, but according to the most recent theories they portray Itzam Cab Aiin, the monster in the form of a caiman that represented the Earth.

THE BIRTH AND RISE
OF A NEW WORLD:
THE POSTCLASSIC PERIOD
(AD 900/1000–1521)

171 - THIS MOSAIC DISK, MADE OF
TURQUOISE AND SHELLS, DEPICTS FOUR
IMAGES OF THE FEATHERED SERPENT; IT IS
FROM CHICHÉN ITZÁ (NATIONAL MUSEUM
OF ANTHROPOLOGY, MEXICO CITY).

172 TOP - THE CASTILLO IS DEDICATED TO
THE CULT OF KUKULKÁN OR THE
FEATHERED SERPENT, THE DEITY THAT WAS
THE CORNERSTONE OF THE POLITICAL
IDEOLOGY THAT SPREAD DURING THE EARLY
POSTCLASSIC PERIOD.

172-173 - THE CASTILLO RISES IN THE
MIDDLE OF THE MAIN SQUARE AT CHICHÉN
ITZÁ. THE TEMPLE OF THE WARRIORS IS
VISIBLE IN THE BOTTOM LEFT, AND THE
BALL COURT IS ON THE RIGHT.

173 - A CHACMOOL AND A THRONE IN
THE SHAPE OF A RED JAGUAR WERE
FOUND ON TOP OF AN OLDER VERSION
OF THE CASTILLO, WHICH WAS LATER
COVERED BY THE MORE RECENT
STRUCTURE OF THE PYRAMID.

The advent of what is known as the Postclassic Period in the Maya area seems to coincide with the crisis of the Puuc cities, i.e., the political entities that enjoyed their greatest development between AD 700 and 1000, at the end of the Classic Period – the very time when their "cousins" to the south declined. One of the factors involved in the crisis of the Puuc Maya was probably the constant influx of groups from the lower Gulf Coast, and particularly the region known as Chontalpa.

The immigration of Chontal Maya groups, described by sources with the names of lineages such as the Itzá and the Xiw, may have contributed to the development of the Puuc region. At this point, however, new migrations triggered social and political mechanisms that led to the collapse of Yucatán centers such as Uxmal, Kabah and Sayil.

The most evident element in these new migrations was the rise of new political ideologies that originated in central Mexico.

Chichén Itzá ("At the Mouth of the Well of the Itzá"), established as a Puuc city, managed to take advantage of these cultural and political conditions, rapidly developing into the largest and most important "Mexicanized" Yucatán capital.

The city became the leading center governed by the Itzá Maya, a group that also settled in other areas of the peninsula (for example Edzná, whose name literally means "The House of the Itzá") and dominated its political scene in close contact with other Maya groups like the Xiw.

Under Itzá rule, the monumental center of Chichén Itzá was renewed with the construction of some of the most impressive buildings in the Maya world, all of which are dis-

tinguished by the iconographic cycles typical of the Toltec culture that dominated central Mexico during this period. The Castillo, an enormous nine-step pyramid was built in the middle of the plaza. The pyramid sustained the temple dedicated to Kukulkán, the Feathered Serpent that was effectively a "translation" of the figure of Quetzalcóatl from central Mexico. Images of the deity were sculpted on the columns of the temple and along the balustrades of a staircase where, during the equinoxes, an optical effect made it look like two large feathered serpents were "descending" from the top of the pyramid.

174-175 - THE TEMPLE OF THE
WARRIORS EFFECTIVELY MERGES THE ART
OF THE MAYA WITH THE TRADITIONS OF
CENTRAL MEXICO. THE TEMPLE WAS
PROBABLY THE FORMAL SEAT OF
GOVERNMENT OF CHICHÉN ITZÁ.

174 BOTTOM LEFT - THE DECORATIVE
FRIEZES ON THE TEMPLE OF THE
WARRIORS DEPICT IMAGES TYPICAL OF
THE ART OF CENTRAL MEXICO, LIKE THIS
PAIR COMPOSED OF AN EAGLE AND A
JAGUAR. THESE ANIMALS MAY HAVE BEEN
THE PATRONS OF SPECIFIC ORDERS OF
WARRIORS.

The Temple of the Warriors is close to the Castillo. This structure, with a broad colonnade next to it, was probably used as the seat of government. In front of the entrance to the temple at the top, flanked by two stately columns depicting feathered serpents, there is a *chacmool*, which was used to collect offerings on the plate set on the statue's lap. Other columns inside the temple are decorated with images of warriors, and the outside walls portray Tlahuizcalpantecuhtli, the war god identified with Venus as the morning star.

The two low platforms in the central plaza also allude

174 BOTTOM RIGHT - THIS BAS-RELIEF
FROM THE OUTER WALL OF THE TEMPLE
OF THE WARRIORS REPRESENTS
TLAHUIZCALPANTECUHTLI, OR VENUS AS
THE MORNING STAR.

175 LEFT - THE CHACMOOL AT THE
ENTRANCE TO THE TEMPLE OF THE
WARRIORS WAS PROBABLY USED TO
RECEIVE RITUAL OFFERINGS ON THE PLATE
SET ON THE STATUE'S LAP. THIS FIGURE
ORIGINATED IN NORTHERN MEXICO
TOWARD THE END OF THE CLASSIC
PERIOD.

175 RIGHT - THE SNOUT OF A FEATHERED
SERPENT SERVES AS THE BASE OF THE
TWO COLUMNS AT THE ENTRANCE TO THE
TEMPLE OF THE WARRIORS. THE SHAFTS,
CARVED TO FORM THE BODY OF A SNAKE,
END WITH A CAPITAL SHAPED LIKE A
RATTLESNAKE.

to warfare: the Venus Platform, decorated with images of Tlahuizcalpantecuhtli, and the Platform of Eagles and Jaguars, where these animals are depicted (probably symbolizing warrior orders) feeding on human hearts obtained through wars and sacrifices.

The largest ball court in Mesoamerica can be seen on the western side of the plaza in Chichén Itzá. It is decorated with a long series of bas-reliefs depicting the two teams and a scene showing a player being beheaded. The Temple of the Jaguars, decorated with bas-reliefs and paintings with war scenes, is annexed to the ball court. The sacred *cenote* after which the city was named is on the north side of the plaza. This enormous karstic well was considered a ritual entry to the world of the water gods, and numerous offerings were thrown into it – from prized ornaments to human beings, whose remains were discovered by archaeologists when they dredged the bottom.

176 TOP - THE PLATFORM OF EAGLES AND JAGUARS IS DECORATED WITH PANELS REPRESENTING EAGLES AND JAGUARS EATING HUMAN HEARTS. THESE ANIMALS REPRESENTED THE WARRIOR ORDERS OF CHICHÉN ITZÁ, BUT THEY ALSO SYMBOLIZED THE TWO OPPOSITE AREAS OF THE COSMOS.

176 BOTTOM - THE VENUS PLATFORM IS DECORATED WITH BAS-RELIEFS THAT DEPICT TLAHUIZCALPANTECUHTLI, OR VENUS AS THE MORNING STAR, PERSONIFIED AS A WARRIOR. THE HEAVENLY POSITIONS OF VENUS OFTEN INDICATED THE MOST FAVORABLE TIME TO GO TO WAR.

176-177 - Two majestic heads of feathered serpents extend from the balustrades of the Venus Platform. The monumental Temple of the Jaguars, annexed to the large ball court at Chichén Itzá, rises in the background.

177 top right - This close-up shows one of the bas-reliefs with a warlike theme decorating the interior of the Annex to the Temple of the Jaguars. It depicts a warrior wearing a feathered "Mexican-style" headdress and accompanied by the figure of a serpent.

177 bottom right - The tzompantli, a wooden rack used to display the skulls of sacrificed prisoners, is decorated with bas-reliefs depicting the long lines of human skulls.

178 TOP LEFT - THIS BAS-RELIEF IS SITUATED ON THE SIDE OF THE BALL COURT AT CHICHÉN ITZÁ. A LAVISHLY DRESSED BALLPLAYER IS SHOWN WITH HIS WIDE BELT-LIKE YOKE AND PROTECTIVE GEAR ON HIS ARMS, AND HE IS CLUTCHING THE RITUAL AXE IN HIS RIGHT HAND.

178 TOP RIGHT - THE BALL DEPICTED IN THE BAS-RELIEF FROM THE BALL COURT AT CHICHÉN ITZÁ BEARS THE IMAGE OF A HUMAN SKULL WITH SMOKE SPIRALING FROM ITS MOUTH.

178-179 - The ball court at Chichén Itzá is the largest in Mesoamerica. Its size indicates that in the Postclassic Period the teams were quite large, unlike the way the game was played during the Classic Period.

179 top - The stone rings mounted along the sides of the ball court and decorated with the images of feathered serpents served as "basketball hoops" through which the players had to pass the rubber ball. These rings were not used until the Postclassic Period and are not present in older ball courts.

179 bottom - The North Temple is visible behind the ball court at Chichén Itzá. To the right is the Temple of the Jaguars, decorated with cycles of polychrome bas-reliefs and murals with war themes, evidently associated with the game.

But why were there so many "Mexican" elements – i.e., elements from central Mexico – in a region that, for millennia, was one of the hubs of the Maya world? For many years, it was thought that Chichén Itzá had effectively been conquered by Toltec groups whose capital, Tula (Hidalgo), had become the leading center of power in central Mexico. According to this theory, the Toltec came to Yucatán with their military leader Quetzalcóatl and established a hybrid Maya-Toltec culture, transforming Chichén Itzá into a "copy" of Tula.

This political model was headed by "government councils" composed of nobles (probably the heads of the various ethnic groups) who were presented as "brothers" and acted under the protection of the Feathered Serpent, the deity that, as the creator of all humanity, represented the perfect linchpin for an ideology that clearly tended toward universalism.

After these new political forms were adopted, Chichén Itzá became the capital of a confederation of cities that probably included various Itzá centers such as Izamal, Mayapán and Edzná,

and that extended its hegemony over much of the Yucatán Peninsula between AD 1000 and 1200. This power was exercised by applying new methods of warfare that were closely connected with the cult of the Feathered Serpent:

However, we now know that Chichén Itzá was never conquered by the Toltec and that the Yucatec Maya, together with the newly arrived Chontal Maya, were the ones who adopted many "Mexican" cultural elements, such as the cult of the Feathered Serpent as well as warfare and models of government.

It seems that these cultural elements were adopted as a result of political demands: the Postclassic Maya needed an ideology suitable for the new multiethnic political entities created as a result of the numerous migrations that occurred when the Classic Period came to an end.

The new social conditions, which were shared by most of Mesoamerica, made dynastic forms of government obsolete. In these dynastic forms, the *ajaw* ruled by virtue of kinship with the founding fathers, governing linguistically uniform populations that political propaganda addressed by means of detailed historical inscriptions. All of this was replaced by a new political model that arose in central Mexico after the fall of Teotihuacán.

wars of conquest fought by large armies and military orders whose martial symbols were the eagle and the jaguar. Their task – at least from an ideological-propagandistic standpoint – was to procure numerous prisoners to be sacrificed. It is no accident that these are the themes we find repeated in the iconographic cycles decorating the buildings around the plaza of the great Yucatec city.

According to historical accounts from later eras, conflicts with the nearby cities of Izamal and Mayapán were ultimately responsible for the fall of Chichén Itzá. Taking advantage of a conflict between the ruler of Chichén Itzá and the one of Izamal, Hunac Ceel, the lord of Mayapán and a descendant of the Cocom, supposedly defeated and sacked Chichén Itzá in 1221 with the help of Mexican or Chontal mercenaries. It is likely that the details of this story are cloaked in legend. Nevertheless, the fact remains that between 1200 and 1250 Chichén Itzá was abandoned, and during this period Mayapán developed into the regional capital.

180 LEFT - THE ANNEX AT THE NUNNERY AND THE CHURCH ARE TWO OF THE BEST-KNOWN PUUC-STYLE BUILDINGS AT CHICHÉN ITZÁ.

180 RIGHT - THE OSSUARY OR HIGH PRIEST'S GRAVE IS A PYRAMID DECORATED WITH IMAGES OF FEATHERED SERPENTS AND CLOUD SERPENTS. BENEATH THE PYRAMID, THERE IS A SMALL NATURAL CAVITY IN WHICH HUMAN REMAINS WERE DISCOVERED.

180-181 - THE CARACOL IS A BUILDING CONNECTED WITH STARGAZING, BUT ITS FUNCTION IS UNCLEAR. IT WAS BUILT TOWARD THE END OF THE CLASSIC PERIOD AND LATER REMODELED.

181 BOTTOM - THE RED HOUSE, WHICH IS SET ON A TALL MONUMENTAL BASE, IS ONE OF CHICHÉN ITZÁ'S PUUC BUILDINGS, AS DEMONSTRATED BY THE INTRICATE MOSAIC FRIEZE THAT DECORATES THE UPPER PART.

THE MAYAPÁN KINGDOM AND ITS DEMISE

The rise of Mayapán under Cocom rule was marked by the continuation of the "Mexican" ways that had already characterized the architecture of Chichén Itzá, but it also reflected the revival of ancient traditions of the peninsular Maya. The Castillo, the city's most important pyramid, was effectively a replica of the pyramid by the same name at Chichén Itzá and, likewise, it was dedicated to the cult of Kukulkán. Other buildings at Chichén Itzá, such as the Caracol and the High Priest's Grave, were also copied at the new capital, which evidently aimed to become a new Tollan. In addition to copying buildings from Chichén Itzá, however, the rulers of Mayapán also built typical Maya monuments, as demonstrated by more than 25 stelae found in this monumental Yucatán center.

The central part of this walled city, composed of about 120 civic and ceremonial buildings, was surrounded by noble residences and over 4000 dwellings. According to archaeological and historical information, Mayapán ruled over a confederation of provinces whose noble elites resided in the monumental center, from which they monitored their lands of origin. This makes it likely that the 13 columned complexes at Mayapán represent the administrative buildings of 13 provinces ruled by the capital.

It seems that Mayapán's wealth was based not only on its control over the various tributary provinces, but also on the intense trade relations established with the lower Gulf Coast and the Guatemalan highlands. The growing importance of long-distance trade, which was one of the most distinctive elements of the Postclassic Maya, seems to have been formed during Mayapán's apogee. The Mayapán kingdom was also short-lived. Toward the middle of the 15th century, the city was sacked and abandoned, probably following an internal revolt headed by a leader of the Tutul Xiw, which culminated with the expulsion of the Cocom and the dissolution of their system of power.

182-183 - MAYAPÁN MANAGED TO FILL THE VACUUM THAT WAS CREATED FOLLOWING THE COLLAPSE OF CHICHÉN ITZÁ, AND IT DOMINATED NORTHERN YUCATÁN BETWEEN AD 1250 AND 1450.

183 TOP - MANY OF THE BUILDINGS IN MAYAPÁN ARE COPIES OF THE ONES AT CHICHÉN ITZÁ. THE CASTILLO DEDICATED TO KUKULKÁN IS VISIBLE IN THE BACKGROUND.

The collapse of Mayapán's centralized power led to a sort of balkanization of the Yucatán political scenario, which was subdivided into numerous independent provinces (there were 16 at the time of the Spanish conquest). Referred to as *cuchcabalob*, they were governed by the nobles of the lineages present in Mayapán, such as the Tutul Xiw, Canul, Cocom, Chel, Tzeh, Cupul and Peh. Despite this political fragmentation, the Yucatec political divisions maintained important trade relations among the peninsular populations and with the Putún or Chontal Maya that controlled the coastal route linking the lower Gulf Coast to the faraway regions of Honduras and El Salvador.

The best archaeological testimony of the wealth of these small provinces comes from the ruins of Tulum (Quintana Roo), the ancient city of Zamá on the east coast of the Yucatán Peninsula. Set in a extraordinarily beautiful landscape, this small walled monumental center is dominated by the Castillo, the temple dedicated to Kukulkán surrounded by other monumental buildings, many of which are reminiscent of the architecture of Mayapán. One of the most important is the Temple of the Frescoes, with paintings portraying typical Maya deities in a pictorial style characteristic of central Mexico (and also found in other peninsular centers such as Santa Rita Corozal) and thus bearing witness to the constant "cultural hybridization" that characterized all the centuries of Postclassic Yucatán.

184 TOP RIGHT - IN THE STATE OF QUINTANA ROO, TULUM — THE ANCIENT CITY OF ZAMÁ — WAS ONE OF THE MOST PROSPEROUS POLITICAL AND COMMERCIAL CENTERS OF THE EAST COAST OF THE YUCATÁN PENINSULA AT THE END OF THE POSTCLASSIC PERIOD. IT WAS STILL A PROSPEROUS CITY WHEN THE SPANISH ARRIVED.

184 CENTER LEFT - THE TEMPLE OF THE FRESCOES IS ONE OF THE MOST FAMOUS BUILDINGS IN TULUM, AND INSIDE IT THERE ARE MURALS WHOSE STYLE CLEARLY REFLECTS THE POWERFUL INFLUENCE OF CENTRAL MEXICO.

184 BOTTOM LEFT - THE MAIN BUILDING
AT TULUM IS THE CASTILLO, ALSO
DEDICATED TO THE CULT OF KUKULKÁN,
DEPICTED ON THE COLUMNS ALONGSIDE
THE ENTRANCE TO THE TEMPLE.

184-185 - THE FORTIFIED CITY OF
TULUM OVERLOOKS THE CARIBBEAN
COAST OF THE YUCATÁN PENINSULA.
CONTROL OF THE COASTAL TRADE
ROUTES, WHICH UNITED THE COAST OF
THE GULF OF MEXICO WITH THE
FARAWAY PORTS ON THE COAST OF
HONDURAS, WAS ONE OF THE MAIN
REASONS THE ANCIENT CITY OF ZAMÁ

186-187 - The famous Madrid Codex is one of the four priceless pre-Hispanic Maya books that escaped destruction. These codices mainly served calendrical, astrological and divinatory purposes (Museum of the Americas, Madrid).

Though most of what we know about the literary culture of the Maya comes from monumental inscriptions, this does not mean that the Maya did not write what we can define as real books. Unfortunately, only four of the thousands of codices – as the ancient Maya books are referred to today – have survived: the Dresden Codex, the Paris Codex, the Madrid Codex and the Grolier Codex, all of which date back to the Late Postclassic Period, or an era after the mid-13th century. Three of the four codices were sent to Europe at the time of the Spanish conquest and were conserved in European libraries; the fourth one (the Grolier Codex) was secretly buried in a dry cave in southern Mexico and was then put on the clandestine market in the mid-1960s.

All four are books composed of strips of paper made from the bark fibers of a type of fig tree, which were covered with lime paste. The prepared strips were then folded accordion-style and enclosed between two covers made of wood or, in some cases, jaguar skins.

The Dresden Codex is undoubtedly the most beautiful and complex of the Maya codices. It probably came from the Yucatán Peninsula, and its 74 pages contain astronomical and ritual texts such as the Venus calendar, eclipse-prediction tables and chapters dedicated to various deities. Based on the sophistication of these images, it seems plausible that the codex must be a copy of an older manuscript that may date back to the Classic Period.

The Grolier Codex, whose authenticity has long been debated, contains a section of the Venus calendar similar to the one in the Dresden Codex, although it was clearly drawn up by a less accomplished scribe.

The Paris Codex, which unfortunately is quite damaged, now consists of 22 pages containing calendar predictions, a description of the creation of the world, and a zodiac.

According to some scholars, the Madrid Codex was drawn up at Tayasal in the 17th century. It is composed of 112 pages containing descriptions of the gods, as well as ritual instructions related to different activities such as hunting, agriculture and beekeeping.

Though all the extant codices date back to the Late Postclassic, we know that similar ones were also produced during the Classic Period. Numerous depictions of codices can be found on the ceramics from the Classic Period, and the remains of codices – unfortunately illegible – have been found at archaeological excavations conducted at various Maya and Mixe-Zoque areas.

186 BOTTOM - THESE PAGES FROM THE MADRID CODEX DEAL WITH RITUAL ACTIVITIES CONNECTED WITH DEER HUNTING. THE PAPER PAGES OF THE CODEX WERE FOLDED ACCORDION-STYLE, WHITENED WITH LIME, AND PAINTED IN BOLD COLORS MADE FROM ORGANIC AND MINERAL PIGMENTS (MUSEUM OF THE AMERICAS, MADRID).

THE MAYA KINGDOMS OF THE HIGHLANDS

A number of independent and warlike kingdoms developed in the highlands of Chiapas and Guatemala during the Postclassic Period. They may have originated through the migration of populations following the collapse of the Classic cities of the lowlands. With the end of the Classic Period, various Maya groups ventured into the highland regions, bringing with them a powerfully Mexicanized Maya culture as a result of contacts with the Putún or Chontal Maya of the Gulf Coast and the Usumacinta Basin.

The most prominent of these groups of invaders were the K'iche', who claimed to descend from the legendary city of Tollan. Through their skillful political and military strategy, they rapidly managed to extend their domain across a broad region of the highlands. According to K'iche' mythology, narrated in the epic cycle of the *Popol Vuh*, the ancestors of this group married into some of the noble families of the highlands, establishing the bloodlines that later came to be known as K'iche', Kaqchikel, Rab'inal and Tz'utujil.

These mythological accounts coincide with archaeological data, indicating Jakawitz as the first K'iche' settlement, founded in about AD 1200. From here, the K'iche' ruler Tz'ikin supposedly conquered the Rab'inal and Iqomaq'i. A few decades after these conquests, the K'iche' moved their capital to Ismachí, where internal conflict led to the division of the three groups that formed K'iche' society. The most noble and powerful of the three groups founded a new capital at Q'umarkaj (Utatlán), led by a ruler who – significantly – was named Q'uq'kumatz, or Feathered Serpent, testifying to the fact that this group shared some of the political models that were most common in Mesoamerica during this period. During his reign and his successor's, the K'iche' managed to extend their control over the entire highland area and to a stretch of the Pacific Coast. It seems that during this era a political organization founded on the coexistence of independent lineages coalesced into a centralized state in which the various lines nevertheless continued to play a key role.

However, the K'iche' political structure soon began to fall apart and the 15th century was marked by the rebellions of the Kaqchikel (who established their own capital at Iximche') and of the Tz'utujil, as well as a series of military campaigns against the Rab'inal, of which we also have literary testimony in the drama entitled *Rab'inal Achi*, set down in 1862 by Charles Etienne Brasseur de Bourbourg.

The K'iche' expansion to the west coast of Guatemala subsequently brought this population into contact with the Aztec, who were conquering the province of Soconusco. These contacts quickly developed into a hierarchical relationship, and in 1510 Q'umarkaj became a tributary of the Aztec Federation, a status it maintained until the Spanish conquest.

The vicissitudes of the K'iche' kingdom in the Guatemalan highlands were paralleled by the development of other centers in the Chiapas highlands, populated by Maya groups such as the Tzotzil, the Tzeltal and the Kanjobal. The most famous of these was Zinacantán, an important trade hub that, even today, is the center of a famous Tzotzil Maya community that has been the subject of some of the most important ethnographic studies of the 20th century.

188-189 - ON THESE TWO PAGES FROM THE MADRID CODEX, THE FIGURE OF CHAC, THE RAIN GOD, IS REPEATED SEVERAL TIMES. THE PICTOGRAPHIC IMAGES ARE ALTERNATED WITH PICTOGRAPHIC-PHONETIC GLYPHS AND NUMERICAL NOTATIONS EXPRESSED WITH BARS AND DOTS (MUSEUM OF THE AMERICAS, MADRID).

191 - THOUGH THE VERSION OF THE *POPOL VUH* KNOWN TO US TODAY DATES BACK TO THE COLONIAL PERIOD, MANY CLASSIC PORTRAYALS REPRESENT SCENES FROM THIS LEGENDARY EPIC. ON THIS PLATE FROM THE CLASSIC PERIOD, WE CAN SEE THE DIVINE TWINS OBSERVING THE MAIZE GOD'S RESURRECTION FROM THE EARTH, WHICH IS DEPICTED AS A TORTOISE (MUSEUM OF FINE ARTS, BOSTON).

When missionaries taught alphabetic writing to the Maya, they certainly could not have imagined that it would be used not only to write prayers and catechisms but also traditional religious texts. As a result, the elite of the colonial Maya groups were able to hand down texts that, had they been preserved in their traditional pictographic form, could easily have been found and destroyed by the Spaniards. The Maya texts that have survived include the *Anales de los Kaqchikeles*, the *Memorial de Sololá*, the *Título de los Señores de Totonicapan*, *The Books of Chilam Balam*, the *Rab'inal Achi* and the *Popol Vuh*. The most famous and important of these texts is unquestionably the *Popol Vuh* ("Council Book"), a mythological text of the K'iche' Maya that was transcribed into alphabetical characters by a priest named Francisco Ximénez. The priest discovered, transcribed and translated this work in the K'iche' city of Chichicastenango between 1701 and 1703. The contents of the book can be divided into three sections. It starts by describing the different attempts to create man, which did not succeed until the fourth try, with the celebrated episode of man's creation from maize. The second part describes the deeds of Hunhapu and Xbalanque, the divine twins who descended to the underworld to play ball against the gods. The third one sets down the history of the K'iche' people, from their legendary origins in the city of Tulán up to the end of the Pre-Hispanic era.

Though the third section is extremely interesting because of the historical reconstruction of the deeds of the Maya from the Guatemalan highlands, the second is certainly the most interesting for studying the Maya culture as a whole. Research into classic iconography has allowed us to understand that the adventures of the twins have been recounted since that period, when these two figures were referred to as Hun Ajaw and Yax B'alam. Comparisons between the scenes illustrated on vases and bas-reliefs and those detailed in the text of the *Popol Vuh* have thus made it possible to study the development and changes that occurred in what must have been the main epic cycle of the ancient Maya civilization.

THE ISTHMIAN AREA DURING THE POSTCLASSIC PERIOD

Current knowledge about the isthmian area during the Postclassic Period is extremely patchy. The region that developed most extensively during this period was Chontalpa, or the lower Gulf Coast, where the Chontal or Putún Maya played a key role in controlling Mesoamerican trade routes. Based in coastal settlements such as the ones at Laguna de Términos and centers such as Itzamkanac, these dynamic traders effectively served as the link between the populations in Veracruz and central Mexico and those of the Yucatán Peninsula. The extensive trade relations of the Putún reached as far as the ports of Nito and Naco, in Honduras, where Putún groups settled permanently to act as terminals for trade relations with their homeland.

The Putún probably had important contacts with the Mixe-Zoque populations along the Veracruz coast, where-

as the territories populated by the Totonac, Otomí, Nahua, Tepehua and Huastec extended to the north.

The Totonac probably reached the Gulf Coast at the end of the Classic Period, but did not manifest the traits distinctive of their culture until the 13th century. Cempoala, the capital of one of the many Totonac kingdoms in Veracruz, was one of the most important Totonac cities. The words that Hernán Cortés and his men wrote about Cempoala and its ruler ("The Fat Cacique") offer us a vibrant description of this city and its lifestyle.

The territory of the Huastec extended to the north of the Totonac region. In the centuries preceding the Spanish conquest, this Maya group, which occupied these lands as far back as the Preclassic Period, enjoyed extraordinary cultural development, exemplified by splendid sculptures that undoubtedly represent one of the high points of

Mesoamerican art. In the southern regions, the Zoque area of western Chiapas was beset by the influx of a foreign Mangue-speaking group, the Chiapanec, who conquered the ancient capital of Chiapa de Corzo and defeated several other Zoque communities, collecting tributes from them.

To escape this pressure, several Zoque groups withdrew to the Selva El Ocote area, reoccupying the ancient settlements that had been abandoned centuries before. The advent of the Chiapanec in Chiapas was evidently part of the sweeping migration process throughout the isthmian area during the Postclassic Period.

The most famous involved the Pipil migration: these Nahua-speaking groups ultimately occupied most of the Pacific coastal areas of Guatemala and El Salvador, going as far as modern-day Nicaragua.

192-193 - The divine twins Hun Ajaw and Yax B'alam are seated before the god Itzamnaj in a vase painting from the Classic Period. The upper inscription gives the Classic names of the two heroes, and also indicates that the vessel was used to drink cocoa (Museum of Fine Arts, Boston).

HISTORY AND TREASURES OF AN ANCIENT CIVILIZATION

THE NEVERENDING CONQUEST
(AD 1519–1697)

Spanish Exploration and Conquest

SPANISH EXPLORATION AND CONQUEST

195 - THIS 16TH-CENTURY MINIATURE DEPICTS HERNÁN CORTÉS LANDING ON THE MEXICAN COAST (BRITISH LIBRARY, LONDON).

196 - THIS ENGRAVING FROM *HISTORIA GENERAL DE LAS INDIAS DI LÓPEZ DE GÓMARA* (1554) DEPICTS FRANCISCO HERNÁNDEZ DE CÓRDOBA'S ARRIVAL IN CUBA IN 1517, THE YEAR HE ALSO BECAME

THE FIRST SPANIARD TO SET FOOT IN MEXICO (NATIONAL LIBRARY, MADRID).

197 - THE PAINTING DEPICTS THE SPANISH EXPLORER AND CONQUEROR JUAN DE GRIJALVA REACHING THE MODERN-DAY REGION OF TABASCO (1517), AT THE MOUTH OF THE RIVER THAT WAS NAMED AFTER HIM (MUSEUM OF THE AMERICAS, MADRID).

Though the history of the populations of southeastern Mesoamerica was always characterized by political upheaval, crisis and military conquests, none of these events were as catastrophic as the arrival of the Spanish *conquistadores* and the subsequent process of material and spiritual conquest to which the native populations were subjected. The Spanish conquest marked the end of Mesoamerica's independent development and the start of a long period of colonial and modern exploitation, which indigenous groups are still struggling to overcome even today.

The first contact between the Maya and the Europeans took place during Christopher Columbus' fourth voyage. In 1502 the Genoese navigator encountered a canoe of Maya traders off the Yucatán coast, an area still unknown to the Old World.

Nine years later, another Spanish ship sank near Yucatán and two survivors, Jerónimo de Aguilar and Gonzalo Guerrero, managed to reach the shore, where they were taken in by the local Maya populations.

The first expedition to the Yucatán Peninsula was conducted in 1517 by Francisco Hernández de Córdoba, who explored the coasts and skirmished with the Maya warriors of Champotón, who wounded him and forced him to flee. The news of a densely populated land led to the organization of another expedition later that year, which set sail from Cuba and was led by Juan de Grijalva. Grijalva explored the Yucatán coast, getting as far as Laguna de Términos, where he was presented with a small amount of gold and told about the Aztec empire.

The news about lands to be conquered, gold and imperial wealth naturally excited the Spaniards, who organized a new expedition of 500 men that set out in 1519, led by Hernán Cortés. Cortés again explored the Yucatán coast, where he met Jerónimo de Aguilar, who joined the expedition as an interpreter (Gonzalo Guerrero refused). Cortés founded a settlement near Potonchán and headed north, commencing the incredible adventure of the conquest of the Aztec empire, which the capable and cynical Spanish captain managed to overthrow in just two years. Once he had conquered México-Tenochtitlan, Cortés turned his attention to the kingdoms along the southern borders of the empire. After ordering an expedition to the coast of Guatemala in 1522, Cortés sent Pedro de Alvarado there. Alvarado reached the area in 1524, and following violent armed clashes he managed to conquer the K'iche' capital of Q'umarkaj, thanks also to the alliance of the Kaqchikel, the traditional rival of the K'iche'. Advised by the Kaqchikel, Alvarado set out toward the Tz'utujil territories, con-

quering their capital city. However, the Kaqchikel never benefited from their alliance with the avid Spanish *conquistador*, who demanded the payment of large tributes. When they revolted against the Spanish in 1526, the Kaqchikel were also defeated and overpowered.

As Alvarado's troops were conquering the Guatemalan highlands, other *conquistadores* ventured into other areas of the Southeast. In 1524 Cortés appointed Captain Luís Marín to conquer the Chiapanec, who had refused to pay tribute. The expedition to Chiapas – supported by many of the populations subject to the Chiapanec – was victorious from a formal standpoint but had few practical repercussions, and Spanish domination remained very weak. Marín also managed to conquer Quechula, one of the most important Zoque centers in the region. Hernán Cortés personally led an expedition through the Petén rainforests. In 1525 he reached Honduras, undertaking the conquest of this area, though this venture was marked above all by rivalry among the Spanish captains.

ē lo dix ē ē̄ ... bēfrs ... 20

melchior diaz mātdio pricipal ē respōd
... ... los ī dios bals y ñolo ē
a cūplir le mādo ē ī hā en el ē cepo dōd
... ē dias

toz puga

altes
miguel
Sanchez

melchior
diez.

melchioz diez
y hpitoca. 8. di.

maçatlagnati   yztacalco. c̄
qui qua
es

m̄ el dr puga. mal ha faua a los
pnagiles in dios ē le ē̄ uian y polen
ut a miguel chichimeca

como la m̄pe del dicho ē dr puga
mal ha ā ā un i dio chalpaçi
ēdo le ē̄ los cabellos y echādole
ē̄ las manos dias malz porā
ē̄ fara buena ē̄ ta

puga

miguel. chichimecatl. topile ē micti
oppa ycaltechtli ē moltac a quez
tihuez

ynamic doctor puga noē micti. y topile miguel chichi
y papa. narasas   amoē quiltta y mi mi me xtin

la m̄pe del
d. puga

No

narasa

In 1526 the Spanish Crown granted Francisco de Montejo permission to conquer Yucatán, which had barely been touched by Cortés' expedition. Montejo set out the following year and gained control over the east coast of the peninsula, using it as a base for a series of military expeditions to the interior, during which he overthrew the rulers of various provinces. His campaign came to a halt in 1528, but the following year Montejo resumed hostilities when, aided by his son Francisco de Montejo the Younger, he conquered the province of Acalan, ruled by the Chontal Maya. The two Montejos subsequently conquered the regions of Campeche and Chetumal, though they also faced a number of difficulties.

In 1527 a new Spanish expedition, headed by Diego de Mazariegos, resumed the campaign to conquer Chiapas. The terrible Battle of Sumidero, where 2000 natives threw themselves into the Sumidero Canyon rather than surrender to the Spaniards, marked the end of Chiapanecan resistance and the start of Spain's complete domination of the area, which culminated with the foundation of Ciudad Real, now called San Cristóbal de Las Casas.

In 1532 Montejo the Younger continued his campaign to conquer the northern part of Yucatán, establishing a Spanish settlement near Chichén Itzá. However, the local Maya, as well as the populations of the provinces that had already been conquered, quickly revolted against the new rulers. The political fragmentation of Yucatán effectively proved to be a significant problem for the Spaniards, as each conquered province quickly rebelled against foreign domination, which in turn was not supported by widespread control over the territory. And when Montejo the Elder took up arms in 1534 to subdue most of the peninsula yet again, his conquest was short-lived.

To make up for the disappointment of the Yucatán expeditions, Montejo the Elder set out to conquer Honduras, as he had been appointed governor of this area in 1535. His son instead resumed his campaign in Yucatán, where he and Lorenzo de Godoy gained control over Champotón, wresting it from the Franciscan Jacobo de Testera, who had begun the peaceful evangelization of the area. Over the years that followed, Montejo the Younger again managed to conquer the northern regions of the peninsula, founding the city of Mérida in 1542. In the meantime, the ongoing conflicts in Honduras also came to an end with the victory of Pedro de Alvarado, who managed to oust Montejo the Elder and definitively take control of the region in 1539.

The occupation of Yucatán effectively ended the conquest of the Southeast, though over the years that followed the Spaniards had to deal with a number of uprisings and conquer several outlying regions that had long managed to avoid Spanish domination. The most famous of these was the city of Tayasal, where the Itzá Maya, led by Canek, managed to maintain their independence until the end of the 17th century. After a number of contacts with Spanish missionaries, the Itzá finally surrendered to the troops of Martín de Ursúa y Arizmendi, who captured the city on March 13, 1697, the date that marks the final conquest of the Maya.

200 - THIS PAGE OF THE CODEX OSUNA (1565) DEPICTS THE ABUSE THE SPANISH INFLICTED ON THE LOCAL POPULATION. NOTABLY, THE MANUSCRIPT COMBINES THE NATIVE PICTOGRAPHIC IMAGES WITH SPANISH TEXTS AS WELL AS NAHUATL TEXTS WRITTEN IN THE LATIN ALPHABET (NATIONAL LIBRARY, MADRID).

201 - THIS PAGE OF THE CODEX OSUNA PORTRAYS TWO NOMADIC HUNTERS FROM NORTHERN MEXICO ARMED WITH BOWS AND ARROWS, WEAPONS TYPICAL OF THE NORTHERN DESERTS. IN THIS CASE, THE STYLE OF THE PAINTED IMAGES ALSO REFLECTS SIGNIFICANT EUROPEAN INFLUENCE (NATIONAL LIBRARY, MADRID).

GLOSSARY

Ah Puch: the name of the Maya death god, portrayed as a skeleton.

Ah ts'ib: the term used in Classic Maya inscriptions to indicate the role of "scribe" or "painter."

Ajaw: "Lord." This was the most common title used in the Classic Maya world. It seems that during the last phases of the Classic Period, this title was also used for top-ranking nobles, even if they were not royalty.

Bacab: one of the names used to refer to the four deities that, according to Classic Maya cosmology, sustained the four corners of the sky.

Baktun: a period of 144,000 days used in the calendar system known as the Long Count.

Calendar Round: the name used to refer to the calendar cycle of 52 years, composed of the combination between the solar calendar of 360 + 5 days and the ritual calendar of 260 days. Unlike the Long Count, this type of cycle was used by all Mesoamerican populations.

Cenote: a natural karstic well created following the partial collapse of the vault of an underground tunnel. These wells, which are very common in karstic areas such as the Yucatán Peninsula, were used for practical purposes – as a water supply – but also for ritual ones, as they were considered accesses to the underworld deities.

Chac: the Maya name of the god of rain and fertility. In Maya iconography, he is portrayed with a long nose resembling an elephant's trunk, but this actually represents the protuberance that various types of snakes have on their snouts.

Cuchcabal: the generic name used for the small political entities of the Maya on the Yucatán Peninsula in the Postclassic period and at the time of contact with the Europeans.

Hun Ajaw: "One Lord," the classic name of one of the divine twins of the epic cycle known as the *Popol Vuh*. In particular, it refers to the elder twin, associated with Venus during the Classic Period. The corresponding name in the colonial version of the *Popol Vuh* is *Hunahpu*.

Hun Naal Ye: the Maize God and the father of the divine twins of the *Popol Vuh*. The Maize God was a leading figure in the mythological cycle closely associated with the sacred legitimization of royalty in the Olmec and Maya world.

Its'at: this term was used in Classic Maya inscriptions to refer to "artist" or "sage." It often appeared in royal titles.

Itzaamnaj: the supreme heavenly deity in the Maya pantheon. He was often portrayed as a toothless old man, but also took the form of a two-headed dragon or a heavenly bird with long feathers.

Itzam Cab Aiin: the earth deity imagined as a caiman whose body floated on underground waters. This deity was also known as *Cipactli* in central Mexico.

K'awiil: this long-nosed god was closely associated with Maya royalty, and was considered a god of royal blood. His image often appeared on royal diadems and on the scepter held by kings, where the god was depicted with a leg in the shape of a snake.

Kaloomté: the Maya royal title used in some cities during the Classic Period. Its exact meaning is not clear yet, but it seems to refer to a higher status than the *ajaw*. When it is associated with the prefix *ochkin* ("western") it can refer to the sovereignty that originated in Teotihuacán.

Katun: a period of 7200 days used in the calendar system known as the Long Count.

K'uhul Ajaw: "Sacred Lord," the royal title most commonly expressed in Classic inscriptions, above all in the so-called Emblem Glyphs, i.e. the ones that seem to refer to the name of the Classic Maya political entities.

Kin: "sun" or "day." As "sun" this term also corresponds to the name of the Maya Sun God, *Kin'ich Ajaw*, recognizable because of distinctive features such as crossed eyes, a curl at the top of his nose and a protruding tongue. As "day" the term corresponds to the shortest period of time (lasting a day) used in the calendar system known as the Long Count.

Kukulkán: "Feathered Serpent" in the Yucatec Maya language. This is a literal translation of the original Nahua name of the god Quetzalcóatl.

Long Count: the calendar system used by the Maya and Mixe-Zoque between the turn of the Preclassic Period and the end of the Classic Period. It is a system that uses different periods of time to calculate the days that have elapsed since a mythical initial date that corresponds to August 13, 3114 BC. The use of this system in Maya monumental inscriptions permits exact correlation with our modern calendar.

Mangue: a Mesoamerican language family. Though Mangue speakers lived outside the isthmus and the Maya area, during the Postclassic Period several Mangue-speaking groups such as the Chiapanec settled in the isthmian area.

Maya: generic name attributed to the speakers of the Mayan or Mayance language family. This language family encompasses about 30 languages, some of which are now extinct.

Mixe-Zoquean: a Mesoamerican language family that includes Mixean and Zoquean. It has been theorized that the ancient Olmec in the metropolitan area spoke a language pertaining to this family.

Nahua: a subgroup of languages pertaining to the large Uto-Aztecan family spoken mainly in central and northern Mexico. This term also refers to Nahua speakers, including the Toltec and the Aztec.

Nahuatl: the Nahua language spoken by the Aztec.

Pawahtun: one of the names used to refer to the four deities that, according to Classic Maya cosmology, sustained the four corners of the sky.

Q'uq'kumatz: "Feathered Serpent" in the K'iche' Maya language. This is a literal translation of the original Nahua name of the god Quetzalcóatl.

Quetzalcóatl: "Feathered Serpent" in Nahuatl. This deity was attributed with various creating activities, including the creation of man. After the end of the Classic Period, this god became the object of a cult that spread throughout Mesoamerica and was closely tied to new and universalistic forms of political power. In fact, the name of the deity – in its different translations – was also adopted as the name of many rulers.

Quincunce: a symbol composed of five points arranged in an X and representing the chief Mesoamerican cosmogram, i.e. the representation of the four cardinal points and the center of the universe.

Sacbe: the "white way" or a road built as a causeway. These roads (*sacbeob* in the plural form) united the various Maya cities and are very common on the Yucatán Peninsula. In addition to serving as communication routes, they were probably used to manifest political relationships between cities. It is likely that they also served a ceremonial purpose.

Sajal: the noble title used in Classic Maya inscriptions to indicate the "governors" of minor centers subject to the authority of an *ajaw*.

Tollan: "Place of Reeds" in Nahuatl. This was the legendary city of Quetzalcóatl that became a mythical urban paradigm. Many Mesoamerican cities such as Tula, Chichén Itzá, Cholula and the Aztec capital of Tenochtitlan were built according to this model.

Tun: "stone" or "year." A period of 360 days used in the calendar system known as the Long Count.

Uinal: a period of 20 days used in the calendar system known as the Long Count.

Yax B'alam: "First Jaguar," the classic name of one of the divine twins of the epic cycle known as the *Popol Vuh*. In particular, it refers to the younger twin, associated with the Sun during the Classic Period. The corresponding name in the colonial version of the *Popol Vuh* is *Xbalanque*.

Adams, Richard. *Prehistoric Mesoamerica, Revised Edition*, Oklahoma University Press, Norman & London 1991.

Benavides Castilli, Antonio et al. *Gli ultimi regni maya*, Jaca Book, Milan 1998.

Clark, John (ed.). *Los olmecas en Mesoamérica*, El Equilibrista, Madrid 1994.

Cobos, Rafael (coord.). *Culto funerario en la sociedad maya*, Memoria de la Cuarta Mesa Redonda de Palenque, INAH, Mexico 2004.

Coe, Michael D. *Breaking the Maya Code*, Thames & Hudson, London 1992.

Coe, Michael D. et al. *The Olmec World. Ritual and Rulership*, Princeton University, Princeton 1995.

Culbert Patrick (ed.). *Classic Maya Political History*, School of American Research Advanced Seminar Series, Cambridge University Press, Cambridge 1991.

Domenici, Davide. *Gli Zoque del Chiapas. Archeologia, storia e antropologia di una millenaria tradizione culturale mesoamericana*, Esculapio, Bologna 2002.

Domenici, Davide. *Mexico*, White Star, Vercelli 2004.

Domenici, Davide. *I linguaggi del potere. Arti e propaganda nell'antica Mesoamerica*, Jaca Book Club, Bologna 2005.

Fash, William. *Scribes, Warriors and Kings. The City of Copán and the Ancient Maya*, Thames & Hudson, London 1991.

Grube, Nikolai (ed.). *Maya: Divine Kings of the Rain Forest*, Könemann, Cologne 2001.

Harrison, Peter D. *The Lords of Tikal. Rulers of an Ancient Maya City*, Thames & Hudson Ltd, London 1999.

Hernandez, A. Arellano, et al. *The Mayas of the Classic Period*, Jaca Book, Milan 1999.

Houston, Stephen. *Maya Glyphs*, British Museum, London 1989.

Manzanilla Linda and Leonardo López Luján. *Historia antigua de México*, 4 vols., Instituto Nacional de Antropología e Historia, Mexico 1994-2000.

Marcus, Joyce. *Mesoamerican Writing Systems. Propaganda, Myth, and History in Four Ancient Civilizations*, Princeton University Press, Princeton 1992.

Martin, Simon and Nikolai Grube. *Chronicle of the Maya Kings and Queens: Deciphering the Dynasties of the Ancient Maya*, Thames & Hudson Ltd, London 2000.

Reents-Budet, Dorie. *Painting the Maya Universe: Royal Ceramics of the Classic Period*, Duke University Press, Durham & London 1994.

Schele, Linda and David Freidel. *A Forest of Kings. The Untold Story of the Ancient Maya*, Quill, New York 1990.

Schele, Linda and Peter Mathews. *The Code of Kings*, Touchstone, New York 1998.

Schele, Linda and Mary Ellen Miller. *The Blood of Kings. Dynasty and Ritual in Maya Art*, Kimbell Art Museum, Fort Worth 1986.

Schmidt, Peter, Mercedes de la Garza and Enrique Nalda (eds.). *Maya*, Rizzoli International Publications, New York 1998.

Sharer, Robert. *The Ancient Maya*, Stanford University Press, Stanford 1994.

Tiesler Blos, Vera, Rafael Cobos and Merle Greene Robertson (coord.). *La organización social entre los mayas*, Memoria de la Tercera Mesa Redonda de Palenque, INAH, Mexico 2002.

Trejo, Silvia (ed.). *Modelos de entidades políticas mayas*, Primer Seminario de Mesas Redondas de Palenque, INAH, Mexico 1998.

Trejo, Silvia (ed.). *Arquitectura e ideologia de los antiguos mayas*, Memoria de la Segunda Mesa Redonda de Palenque, INAH, Mexico 2000.

Trejo, Silvia (ed.). *La guerra entre los antiguos mayas*, Memoria de la Primera Mesa Redonda de Palenque, INAH, Mexico 2000.

Webster, David. *The Fall of the Ancient Maya: Solving the Mystery of the Maya Collapse*, Thames & Hudson, London 2002.

Aisa: pages 47, 49, 90, 108, 128, 140-141, 166, 186, 186-187, 188-189, 197, 199, 200, 201

Antonio Attini/Archivio White Star: pages 33 right, 55, 82-83, 84, 92-93, 93 top and bottom, 105, 109

Archivio Iconografico S.A./Corbis: page 126

Archivio Scala: pages 62-63, 69 left and right

Archivio White Star: pages 10-11, 91 left

Yann Arthus-Bertrand/Corbis: pages 6-7, 155, 172, 172-173

Michael Blake: page 24

Massimo Borchi/Archivio White Star: pages 1, 8, 20-21, 80, 81, 104-105, 107 left, 112, 112-113, 113 top and bottom, 114 top and bottom, 114-115, 124 top and bottom, 125 top and bottom, 134 top and bottom left and right, 134-135, 135 bottom, 138, 139 left, center and right, 154, 154-155, 157 top, 160 top and bottom, 161, 162-163, 163 top, center left and right, 163 bottom, 164-165, 165, 168 top and bottom, 168-169, 173, 174-175, 174 bottom left and right, 175 left and right, 176 top and bottom, 176-177, 177 right top and bottom, 178 top left and right, 178-179, 179 top and

bottom, 180 left and right, 180-181, 181, 184 top, center and bottom, 184-185

Bridgemnan Art Library/Archivio Alinari: page 27, 149 bottom

British Museum: pages 62, 63

Richard A. Cooke/Corbis: page 29

Gianni Dagli Orti/Art Archive: pages 56, 57 left and right, 64, 67, 77, 78, 79, 146-147, 196, 198

Gianni Dagli Orti/Corbis: pages 23, 31, 44 right, 51

Pierre-Yves Dhinaut: page 96 left and right

Raphael Doniz: page 45

Macduff Everton/Corbis: pages16-17, 136-137, 141

Elisabetta Ferrero/Archivio White Star: page 15

Werner Forman/Corbis: page 129

Damm Fridmar/Sime/Sie: pages 106-107

Kenneth Garrett: pages 30-31, 32-33, 58 top and bottom, 58-59, 60-61,86 left, 110-111, 117, 122 top, 142-143

Javier Hinoyosa: pages 2-3, 25, 33 left, 36, 37 left and right, 38, 39, 48 top and bottom, 54, 70-71, 74 top and

bottom, 75 top and bottom left and right, 86, 87, 88, 89, 101 left and right, 118 left and right, 119, 120, 121, 148-149, 150, 151, 156-157, 157 bottom, 158 top and bottom, 158-159, 182-183

Barbara Kerr: page 183

Justine Kerr: pages 26, 40, 40-41, 42, 43, 65, 96-97, 122 bottom, 123, 130, 132-133, 144-145, 191, 192-193

Danny Lehman/Corbis: pages 28, 116-117

Charles & Josette Lenars/Corbis: pages 4-5, 94-95, 95, 142 bottom

Erich Lessing Archive/Contrasto: pages 34, 35, 44 left, 52-53, 68, 98 right, 102, 103, 131, 146, 152, 153 left and right, 167, 195

Craig Lovell/Corbis: page 142 top

Photoservice Electa/Akg-images: pages 13, 72, 73, 91 right, 98 left, 99 left and right, 100 left and right, 127, 136

Kevin Schafer/Corbis: pages 124-125

Linda Schele: page 50 (drawing)

Henri Stierlin: pages 171, 208

Werner Formar Archive: page 144

Nik Wheeler/Corbis: pages 18-19

208 - THE TABLET OF THE SLAVES FROM PALENQUE (AD 730) IS AN EXCELLENT EXAMPLE OF THE LEVEL OF SOPHISTICATION ACHIEVED BY MAYA ARTISTS.